직독직해로 읽는

셜록 홈즈 걸작선

The Five Orange Pips /

The Adventure of the Blue Carbuncle

직독직해로 읽는
셜록 홈즈 걸작선

The Five Orange Pips /
The Adventure of the Blue Carbuncle

개정판 2쇄 발행 2019년 4월 10일
초판 1쇄 발행   2014년 1월 20일

원작   아서 코넌 도일
역주   더 콜링(김정희, 박윤수)
디자인   IndigoBlue
일러스트 정은수
발행인   조경아
발행처   랭귀지북스
주소   서울시 마포구 포은로2나길 31 벨라비스타 208호
전화   02.406.0047   **팩스**   02.406.0042
이메일   languagebooks@hanmail.net
홈페이지 www.languagebooks.co.kr
등록번호 101-90-85278   **등록일자** 2008년 7월 10일
ISBN   979-11-5635-056-9 (13740)
가격   12,000원

blog.naver.com/languagebook에서 MP3 파일을 다운로드할 수 있습니다.

이 도서의 국립중앙도서관 출판예정도서목록(CIP)은 서지정보유통지원시스템 홈페이지(http://seoji.nl.go.kr)와
국가자료공동목록시스템(http://www.nl.go.kr/kolisnet)에서 이용하실 수 있습니다. (CIP제어번호 : CIP2016028794)

직독직해로 읽는

셜록 홈즈 걸작선

The Five Orange Pips /
The Adventure of the Blue Carbuncle

아서 코넌 도일 원작

더 콜링 역주

Language Books

머리말

"어렸을 때 누구나 갖고 있던 세계명작 한 질.
그리고 TV에서 하던 세계명작 만화에 대한 추억이 있습니다."

"친숙한 이야기를 영어 원문으로 읽어 봐야겠다고 마음 먹고 샀던 원서들은
이제 애물단지가 되어 버렸습니다."

"재미있는 세계명작 하나 읽어 보려고 따져 보는 어려운 영문법,
모르는 단어 찾느라 이리저리 뒤져 봐야 하는 사전.
몇 장 넘겨 보기도 전에 지칩니다."

영어 독해력을 기르려면 술술 읽어가며 내용을 파악하는 것이 중요합니다. 현재 수능 시험에도 대세인 '직독직해' 스타일을 접목시킨 〈직독직해로 읽는 세계명작 시리즈〉는 세계명작을 영어 원작으로 쉽게 읽어갈 수 있도록 안내해 드릴 것입니다.

'직독직해' 스타일로 읽다 보면, 영문법을 들먹이며 따질 필요가 없으니 쉽고, 끊어 읽다 보니 독해 속도도 빨라집니다. 이 습관이 들여지면 어떤 글을 만나도 두렵지 않을 것입니다.

명작의 재미를 즐기며 영어 독해력을 키우는 두 마리의 토끼를 잡으세요!

〈직독직해로 읽는 세계명작 시리즈〉의 나의 소중한 파트너이자 오랜 친구 윤수, 늘 한결같이 성실하게 그림을 그려 주시는 일러스트레이터 은수 씨, 좋은 멘토 디자인 IndigoBlue, 그리고 이 책이 출판될 수 있도록 늘 든든하게 지원해 주시는 랭귀지북스에 감사의 마음을 전합니다.

마지막으로 내 삶의 이유가 되시는 하나님께 영광을 올려 드립니다.

더 콜링 김정희

목차

Episode 1 : The Five Orange Pips

C O N T E N T S

Episode 2 : The Adventure of
　　　　　　　the Blue Carbuncle

읽기 가이드

영어 앞에만 서면 숨이 콱콱 막힌다…
〈직독직해로 읽는 〈세계 명작〉 시리즈와 함께하세요!

I

어떻게 하면 어려워 보이는 영어 명작을 술술 읽을 수 있을
까요?
우선 문제점부터 살펴봅시다.

(1) 배웠던 문법 따져가며 읽지 않았나요?

관계대명사절부터 to 부정사 어쩌구 저쩌구… 저절로 골치가 아파옵니
다. 재미있게 읽어볼까 하고 폈던 책을 덮어버리고 맙니다. 골치 아픈 문
법을 따지다 보면 정작 책에서 놓치지 말아야 할 중요한 '내용'은 무엇
인지 감도 잡히지 않습니다.

(2) 뒤에 수식구 찾고 앞에 주어 찾고 왔다갔다 정신없이 읽었나요?

들인 시간에 비해 진도는 몇 장 안 나가고, 그렇게 명작의 재미를 찾지
못하고, 결국 지치고 맙니다. 앞뒤로 왔다갔다 하면서 읽는 것은 시간 낭
비뿐 아니라 의욕 상실의 주범입니다.

II

그럼 어떻게 하면 재미도 있고, 쭉쭉 읽어갈 수 있을까요?

(1) 그래서 제시하는 방법이 직독직해입니다.

현재 수능에서도 직독직해가 대세인만큼 독해 실력의 향상을 위해서 꼭
필요한 방법입니다.

아무리 복잡하고 긴 글이라도, 문법을 따지기 보다는 전체적인 내용 이
해에 중점을 두며 읽는 방법, 즉 '나무보다 숲'을 보는 방법입니다.

직독직해가 익숙해지면, 그 동안 어려웠던 영문 소설이 어느 새 쉽게 다
가올 것입니다.

(2) 직독직해를 잘하려면 끊어 읽기를 잘해야 합니다.

그럴려면 영어 문장의 구조에 대한 지식이 필요합니다. 무작정 끊어 읽
기를 한다면, 어디에서 끊어야 할지도 모르고 대충 끊어 읽어서 의미의
연결이 어렵습니다.

III
그러면 어디에서 끊어야 할까요?

(1) 주어가 길면
→ 전체 주어 묶음 뒤에서 끊습니다.

What is done / cannot be undone.
일어난 일은 / 되돌릴 수 없다.

That I have done / is important thing.
내가 했다는 것은 / 중요한 일이다.

(2) 타동사 뒤에 목적어로 명사 또는 대명사가 나오면
→ 그 뒤에서 끊습니다.

We opened it / immediately.
우리는 그것을 열었다 / 바로.

He put his hand / in his pocket.
그는 손을 넣었다 / 주머니 안에.

⑶ 타동사 뒤에 목적어의 묶음이 길게 오면

→ 목적어 앞에서 끊습니다.

But she could not understand / why Sara looked different.

하지만 그녀는 이해할 수 없었다 / 왜 새라가 달라졌는지.

People refuse to believe / that a strange new thing can be done.

사람들은 믿기 거부했다 / 낯설고 새로운 것들이 이루어질 수 있다는 것을.

(4) 수식어구를 만난다면
→ 전치사+명사의 묶음 앞에서 끊습니다.

Men / in shirt sleeves / were going in and out.

남자들이 / 셔츠 차림의 / 들락날락 하고 있었다.

The small drudge / brfore the grate / swept the hearth once.

어린 하녀는 / 난로 앞에 있던 / 난로 바닥을 한 번 쓸었다.

→ 명사+ 현재분사/과거분사/형용사의 묶음 앞에서 끊습니다.

A huntsman / returning with his dogs / from the field, / fell in by chance / with a Fisherman.

한 사냥꾼이 / 개들을 끌고 돌아오던 / 들판에서 / 우연히 마주쳤다 / 낚시꾼과.

The shrpest needle / warranted not to cut in the eye / was not sharper the Scrooge.

가장 날카로운 바늘도 / 바늘귀가 부러지지 않는다고 보장된 / 스크루지보다 날카롭지 못했다.

→ 명사+관계사의 묶음 앞에서 끊습니다.

Martha / who was a poor apprentice at a milliner's / told them.

마사는 / 숙녀용 모자가게에서 일하는 가난한 견습공인 / 그들에게 말했다.

Two men / who watched the light / had made a fire.

두 남자가 / 빛을 지키는 / 불을 지폈다.

⑸ 부사절과 주절이 있다면

→ 그 경계에서 끊습니다.

부사절의 위치는 주절의 앞에 놓일 수도 있고, 뒤에 놓일 수도 있습니다. 부사절의 위치와 상관없이 경계에서 끊고, 부사절과 주절은 서로 독립된 문장 구조를 갖기 때문에 완전히 별도로 해석해야 합니다.

As he was crossing through the water / he lost his footing.

물을 건너고 있을 때 / 그는 발을 헛디뎠다.

A carter was driving a wagon / along a country lane, / when the wheels sank down deep / into a rut.

마부가 마차를 몰고 있었다 / 시골길을 따라, / 그때 바퀴가 깊게 빠져버렸다 / 바퀴 자국에.

(6) to부정사가 '~하기 위해서'라고 해석된다면

→ to 부정사 앞에서 끊습니다.

It took two hands / to do it.

두 손이 필요했다 / 그것을 하기 위해.

She looked behind her / up the long walk / to see if anyone was coming.

그녀는 뒤를 돌아다 보았다 / 긴 산책로 끝을 / 누가 오고 있는지 보기 위해.

이 외에도 여러 가지 방법이 있습니다.
하지만 언어는 수학처럼 공식에 맞춰 공부할 수 없습니다.
탄력성 있게 그 언어가 가지고 있는 매력을 느끼는 것이
가장 중요합니다. 이 모든 방법은 의미가 잘 통하기
위함이라는 것을 명심하세요!
그럼 〈직독직해로 읽는 〈세계 명작〉 시리즈와 함께
즐거운 영어 공부를 시작해 보세요!

Episode 1

The Five Orange Pips

다섯 개의 오렌지 씨앗

1

When I glance over / my notes and records of the
훑어보면 / 셜록 홈즈의 사건에 대한 내 기록을

Sherlock Holmes cases / between the years '82 and '90,
1882년부터 1890년까지의,

/ I am faced by so many / which present strange and
너무 많은 사건이 있어서 / 기이하고 흥미로운 특징을 보여 주는

interesting features / that it is no easy matter / to know /
쉬운 일은 아니다 / 알아내기가

which to choose / and which to leave. Some, / however,
어느 것을 고르고 / 어느 것을 버려야 할지. / 일부 사건은, 하지만,

/ have already gained publicity / through the papers, /
이미 유명세를 얻었지만 / 신문 기사를 통해,

and others have not offered / a field for those peculiar
다른 사건들은 보여 주지 못했다 / 특이한 특징들을

qualities / which my friend possessed / in so high a
내 친구가 가지고 있는 / 그토록 대단하게,

degree, / and which it is the object of these papers / to
이런 글의 목적임에도 / 그것을

illustrate. Some, / too, / have baffled his analytical skill,
보여 주는 것이. / 어떤 사건은, 또, / 홈즈의 분석력으로도 이해할 수 없기에,

/ and would be, / as narratives, / beginnings without an
그래서, / 이야기가 될 터였다, / 시작만 하고 끝을 맺지 못하는,

ending, / while others have been but partially cleared
반면 다른 사건들은 일부만 해결되어서,

up, / and have their explanations founded / rather upon
그런 사건은 설명해야 한다

conjecture and surmise / than on that absolute logical
추측과 추정에 기초하여, / 완벽한 논리적 증거가 아니라

proof / which was so dear to him. There is, however, /
홈즈가 그토록 소중히 여기는. / 그러나, 있다

one of these last / which was so remarkable in its details
후자에 해당하는 사건 하나가 / 사건 내용이 매우 놀랍고

/ and so startling in its results / that I am tempted to give
결과가 특이해서   설명하고 싶은 유혹을 느끼는

some account of it / in spite of the fact / that there are
                          사실에도 불구하고   내용이 있다는

points / in connection with it / which never have been, /
사건과 관련하여   아직 되지 않았고,

and probably never will be, / entirely cleared up.
앞으로 되지 못할 것 같은,   완전한 해결이.

Key Expression 🔑

in spite of : ~에도 불구하고

in spite of는 '~에도 불구하고'라는 뜻을 가진 전치사구입니다. in spite of 와 같은 뜻을 가진 단어로 despite가 있습니다. in spite of와 despite는 모두 전치사이기 때문에 뒤에는 명사나 명사구가 와야 합니다.
뒤에 문장이 오기 위해서는 in spite of the fact that처럼 동격의 that 절을 사용하거나, 같은 의미를 가진 접속사인 though나 although를 써야 합니다.

▶ in spite of + 명사
▶ despite + 명사
▶ though + 주어 + 동사
▶ although + 주어 + 동사
▶ in spite of[despite] the fact that + 주어 + 동사

ex) I am tempted to give some account of it in spite of the fact that there are
points in connection with it which never have been, and probably never will
be, entirely cleared up.
사건과 관련해 아직 완전히 해결되지 않았고 아마 앞으로도 되지 않을 것 같은
점들이 있다는 사실에도 불구하고 설명하고 싶은 유혹을 느낀다.
But in spite of the help of several passers-by, it was quite impossible to effect
a rescue.
하지만 지나가던 행인들의 도움에도 불구하고, 구조는 불가능했다.
We found the brass box there, although its contents had been destroyed.
내용물은 망가져 버렸지만, 그곳에서 놋쇠함을 발견했죠.

glance 흘낏 보다 | publicity 언론의 주목 | peculiar 기이한 | baffle 좌절시키다, 이해할 수 없다 | analytical
분석적인 | conjecture 추측 | surmise 추측, 추정 | startling 특이한

The year '87 furnished us / with a long series of cases /
1887년에는 있었다   많은 사건들이 연이어

of greater or less interest, / of which I retain the records.
대단한 사건부터 신통치 않은 사건까지,   내가 보유한 사건 중에는.

Among my headings / under this one twelve months
사건 제목 중에는   그 해 열두 달 동안

/ I find an account of the adventure of the Paradol
패러들 챔버 사건이 있고,

Chamber, / of the Amateur Mendicant Society, / who
아마추어 탁발 협회 사건,

held a luxurious club / in the lower vault of a furniture
호화로운 모임을 열었던   가구 창고 지하실에서,

warehouse, / of the facts connected with the loss / of
분실 사건과 관련된 기록

the British barque "Sophy Anderson", / of the singular
영국 범선   '소피 앤더슨 호'에서 일어난,

adventures of the Grice Patersons / in the island of Uffa,
그라이스 패터슨이 겪은 신기한 모험   우파 섬에서,

/ and finally of the Camberwell poisoning case. In the
그리고 마지막으로 캠버웰 독극물 사건이 있다.   캠버웰 사건

latter, / as may be remembered, / Sherlock Holmes was
에서는,   기억이 생생한,   셜록 홈즈는 가능했다,

able, / by winding up the dead man's watch, / to prove /
죽은 사람의 시계 태엽을 감아서,   밝혀내는 것이

that it had been wound up / two hours before, / and that
시계 태엽이 감겼으며   두 시간 전에,

therefore the deceased had gone to bed / within that time
따라서 죽은 사람이 잠자리에 든 것은   두 시간 전 이내라는 것을

/ — a deduction which was of the greatest importance /
— 이 추리는 중요한 역할을 했다

in clearing up the case.
그 사건을 밝혀내는 데.

All these / I may sketch out / at some future date, / but
이 모든 사건은　소개할지도 모르지만　앞으로 언젠가,

none of them present / such singular features as the
그 어느 사건도 보여 주지 못한다

strange train of circumstances / which I have now taken
이토록 독특한 특징의 정황을

up my pen to describe.
내가 지금 설명하려고 펜을 든 사건만큼.

It was in the latter days of September, / and the
때는 9월 말이었고,

equinoctial gales had set in / with exceptional violence.
추분의 강풍이 불었다　유례없이 세차게.

All day / the wind had screamed / and the rain had
하루 종일　바람이 울부짖었고

beaten against the windows, / so that even here / in the
비가 창문을 거세게 때렸다,　그래서 이곳에서도

heart of great, hand-made London / we were forced to
거대한 인공의 도시 런던 심장부에 있는

raise our minds / for the instant / from the routine of life
정신을 차리고　잠시 동안　일상 생활에서 벗어나

/ and to recognise / the presence of those great elemental
인식할 수밖에 없었다　위대한 대자연의 존재를

forces / which shriek at mankind / through the bars of
인류를 향해 비명을 지르는

his civilisation, / like untamed beasts in a cage.
문명이라는 철창 사이로,　우리에 갇힌 야수처럼.

furnish 제공하다 | retain 유지하다 | vault 보관실 | barque 바크형 범선(돛대가 세 개 이상인 범선) |
equinoctial 춘분, 추분의 | gale 강풍, 돌풍 | recognise 인식하다(=recognize) | shriek 비명를 지르다 |
civilisation 문명(=civilization)

As evening drew in, / the storm grew higher and louder,
저녁이 다가오자, 폭풍우는 점점 더 거세져서,

/ and the wind cried and sobbed / like a child in the
바람 소리가 울부짖는 듯 했다 굴뚝에 갇힌 아이처럼.

chimney. Sherlock Holmes sat moodily / at one side
셜록 홈즈는 침울하게 앉아서

of the fireplace / cross-indexing his records of crime, /
벽난로 가에 범죄 기록을 검토하고 있었고,

while I at the other / was deep in one of Clark Russell's
난 맞은편에서 클라크 러셀의 멋진 바다 이야기에 빠져 있어

fine sea-stories / until the howl of the gale from without /
바람이 울부짖는 소리가 어디에서 오는지

seemed to blend with the text, / and the splash of the rain
책 내용과 섞이는 듯 했고, 빗방울 튀는 소리가

to lengthen out / into the long swash of the sea waves.
파도가 부서지는 소리처럼 들렸다.

My wife was on a visit to her mother's, / and for a few
아내는 장모님을 뵈러 갔기에, 며칠 동안

days / I was a dweller / once more / in my old quarters at
난 지내고 있었다 다시 한 번 베이커 가의 옛 하숙집에서.

Baker Street.

"Why," / said I, / glancing up at my companion, / "that
"여보게," 내가 말했다, 친구를 올려다 보며,

was surely the bell. Who could come to-night? Some
"초인종 소리인 것 같은데. 이 밤에 누가 온 거지?

friend of yours, / perhaps?"
자네 친구들인가, 아마도?"

"Except yourself / I have none," / he answered.
"자네 말고 내게 친구는 없네," 그가 대답했다.

"I do not encourage visitors."
"난 손님이 찾아오는 걸 반기지 않으니."

"A client, / then?"
"의뢰인인가, 그럼?"

chimney 굴뚝 | moodily 침울하게 | cross-index 상호 참조 표시를 하다 | howl 울부짖다 | splash 첨벙 하는
소리 | swash 쏴파, 파도가 부서진 물살 | dweller 거주자 | quarter 숙소, (도시 내의) 구역

"If so, / it is a serious case. Nothing less would bring
그렇다면, 심각한 사건이겠군.   사람이 밖에 나오진 않을 테니

a man out / on such a day and at such an hour. But I
이런 날씨와 이런 시간에.   내 생각에

take it / that it is more likely to be some crony of the
주인 아주머니의 친구같은데."

landlady's."

Sherlock Holmes was wrong in his conjecture, /
셜록 홈즈의 추리는 틀렸다,

however, / for there came a step in the passage / and
그러나,   왜냐하면 복도에 발 소리가 들리더니

a tapping at the door. He stretched out his long arm /
문을 두드리는 소리가 났으니까.   그는 긴 팔을 뻗어

to turn the lamp away from himself / and towards the
자신을 향해 있었던 램프를 돌려서   빈 의자를 향해 놓았다

vacant chair / upon which a newcomer must sit.
손님이 앉게 될.

"Come in!" / said he.
"들어오시오!"   그가 말했다.

The man who entered was young, / some two-and-
들어온 남자는 젊은이로, 스물 둘 셋 정도로,

twenty at the outside, / well-groomed and trimly clad,
단정하고 깔끔한 차림에,

/ with something of refinement and delicacy in his
세련되고 섬세한 태도의 청년이었다.

bearing. The streaming umbrella / which he held in his
물이 떨어지는 우산을 손에 들고,

hand, / and his long shining waterproof / told of the
긴 비옷이 반짝이는 모습으로

fierce weather / through which he had come. He looked
험한 날씨를 알려 주었다 그가 뚫고 온. 그는 불안해 하며

about him anxiously / in the glare of the lamp, / and I
주위를 둘러보았고 램프의 불빛 속에서,

could see / that his face was pale / and his eyes heavy,
보였다 얼굴은 창백하고 눈빛은 심각하게,

/ like those of a man who is weighed down / with some
짓눌려 있는 사람처럼

great anxiety.
큰 걱정거리에.

"I owe you an apology," / he said, / raising his golden
"사과 드리겠습니다." 그가 말했다, 금색 코안경을 올리며.

pince-nez to his eyes.

"I trust that I am not intruding. I fear that I have brought
"폐를 끼칠 생각은 없었습니다. 가져와 버려 죄송합니다

/ some traces of the storm and rain / into your snug
폭풍우의 흔적을

chamber."
아늑한 방 안에."

"Give me your coat and umbrella," / said Holmes.
"외투와 우산을 주시죠," 홈즈가 말했다.

---

crony 친구 | well-groomed 차림새가 단정한 | trimly 정돈하여 | clad ~을 입은 | refinement 개선 |
delicacy 섬세함 | bearing 태도, 자세 | anxiously 걱정스럽게 | weigh down 짓누르다 | anxiety 불안 |
pince-nez 코안경 | intrude 방해하다 | snug 포근한, 아늑한

"They may rest here on the hook / and will be dry
"여기 옷걸이에 걸어두면 곧 마를 겁니다.

presently. You have come up / from the south-west, / I
오셨군요 남서부에서

see."
보아하니."

"Yes, from Horsham."
"네, 호셤에서요."

"That clay and chalk mixture / which I see upon your toe
"점토와 석회가 구두 앞 코에 묻어 있는

caps / is quite distinctive."
매우 특이하니까요."

"I have come for advice."
"조언을 들으러 왔습니다."

"That is easily got."
"그거야 쉬운 일이지요."

"And help."
"그리고 도움도."

"That is not always so easy."
"그건 쉽지 않을 때도 있지요."

"I have heard of you, / Mr. Holmes. I heard from Major
"선생에 대한 이야기를 들었습니다, 홈즈 씨. 프렌더개스트 소령님께 들었습니다

Prendergast / how you saved him / in the Tankerville
그를 구해 주셨다고 탱커빌 클럽 사건에서."

Club scandal."

"Ah, of course. He was wrongfully accused / of cheating
"아, 그렇군요. 소령은 누명을 썼지요 속임수를 쓴다고

/ at cards."
카드 게임에서."

"He said / that you could solve anything."
"말씀하셨어요 선생은 어떤 일이든 해결할 수 있다고."

"He said too much."
"과찬입니다."

"That you are never beaten."
"그리고 결코 지는 일이 없다고요."

"I have been beaten four times / — three times by men, /
"네 번 실패했습니다   — 세 번은 남자에게,

and once by a woman."
그리고 한 번은 여자에게."

"But what is that compared / with the number of your
"하지만 비교해 보면 어떤가요   성공한 횟수에?"

successes?"

"It is true / that I have been generally successful."
"사실입니다   대부분 성공했다는 사실은."

"Then you may be so with me."
"그럼 제 문제도 성공하시겠지요."

"I beg that you will draw your chair / up to the fire / and
"의자를 당겨서 앉으시고   난로 가까이

favour me with some details / as to your case."
자세히 얘기해 보시오   사건에 대해.

"It is no ordinary one."
"평범한 사건은 아닙니다."

"None of those which come to me are. I am the last court
"내게 찾아오는 사건은 어느 것도 평범하지 않습니다.   나는 마지막으로 호소하는

of appeal."
대법원 같은 존재지요.

"And yet / I question, sir, / whether, / in all your
"하지만   궁금하군요   있는지,

experience, / you have ever listened to / a more
선생의 경험에서,   들어본 적이

mysterious and inexplicable chain of events / than those
더 기이하고 설명할 수 없는 사건을

which have happened in my own family."
우리 가족에게 일어난 사건보다."

---

chalk 백악(백색 연토질 석회암) | distinctive 독특한 | as to ~에 대해 | inexplicable 불가해한, 설명할 수 없는

"You fill me with interest," / said Holmes.
"흥미롭군요," 홈즈가 말했다.

"Pray give us the essential facts / from the
"중요한 사실을 말해 주시오 처음부터,

commencement, / and I can afterwards question you
그리고 나서 질문하겠소

/ as to those details / which seem to me to be most
세부 사항에 대해 가장 중요해 보이는."

important."

The young man pulled his chair up / and pushed his wet
젊은이는 의자를 당기고 젖은 발을 쭉 뻗었다

feet out / towards the blaze.
불 쪽으로.

"My name," / said he, / "is John Openshaw, / but my own
"제 이름은," 그가 말했다. "존 오픈쇼입니다, 하지만 제 자신에

affairs have, / as far as I can understand, / little to do
대한 사항은, 제가 아는 한,

with this awful business. It is a hereditary matter; / so in
이 끔찍한 사건과 관련이 없습니다. 이건 상속과 관련된 문제입니다;

order to give you an idea of the facts, / I must go back /
그래서 그 사실에 대해 알려 드리기 위해, 거슬러 올라가야겠군요

to the commencement of the affair.
사건의 발단으로.

Key Expression ♥

as far as : ~하는 한
as far as는 부사절을 이끄는 접속사로 '~하는 한'이라는 뜻을 가지고 있습니다.
또한 거리를 나타내어 '~와 같은 거리까지'라는 의미를 나타낼 때도 있습니다.

ex) My own affairs have, as far as I can understand, little to do with this awful
business.
제가 아는 한, 제 자신에 대한 사항은 이 끔찍한 사건과 관련이 없습니다.

You must know / that my grandfather had two sons / —
아셔야 합니다　　　　할아버지에겐 두 아들이 있었다는 사실을

my uncle Elias / and my father Joseph. My father had a
— 엘리아스 큰아버지와　제 아버지인 조셉입니다.　　아버지는 작은 공장을 운영

small factory / at Coventry, / which he enlarged / at the
하셨는데　　　　코번트리에서,　　사업을 확장하셨죠

time of the invention of bicycling. He was a patentee / of
자전거가 발명될 때.　　　　　　　아버지는 특허권을 가졌기에

the Openshaw unbreakable tire, / and his business met
오픈쇼 타이어의,　　　　　　사업은 성공적이었고

with such success / that he was able to sell it / and to
그래서 공장을 팔아서

retire upon a handsome competence.
상당한 돈을 손에 넣고 은퇴할 수 있었지요.

My uncle Elias emigrated to America / when he was a
큰아버지는 미국으로 이민 가서　　　　　　　젊었을 때

young man / and became a planter in Florida, / where
플로리다에서 농장을 운영하셨는데,

he was reported to have done very well. At the time of
그곳에서 성공하셨다는 소식이 들렸죠.　　　　남북전쟁 때

the war / he fought in *Jackson's army, / and afterwards
잭슨 장군 아래에서 싸우셨고,　　　　　나중에는 후드 장군 밑으

under Hood, / where he rose to be a colonel. When
로 가서,　　　대령까지 오르셨어요.

**Lee laid down his arms / my uncle returned to his
리 장군이 항복하자　　　큰아버지는 농장으로 돌아가,

plantation, / where he remained / for three or four years.
그곳에 머무셨어요　　3~4년 동안.

* 토머스 조너선 잭슨. 미국 남북 전쟁 시대 로버트 리 장군의 심복이었던 남부 연합의 장군으로 눈
부신 전투로 인해 '스톤월 잭슨' 이라 불렸다.
** 로버트 리. 미국의 군인이자 교육자로 남북전쟁 당시 남부군에 참가하여 버지니아 주 지휘를 맡
았으며 남부연합 대통령 J.데이비스의 군사고문 및 군사령관이었다.

commencement 시작, 개시 | blaze 화재 | hereditary 세습되는 | patentee 특허권자 | retire upon a
handsome competence 상당한 돈을 손에 넣고 은퇴하다 | emigrate 이민을 가다, (다른 나라로) 이주하다 |
planter 농장주 | plantation (대규모) 농장

About 1869 or 1870 / he came back to Europe / and took
1869년인가 1870년에 유럽으로 돌아와서

a small estate / in Sussex, near Horsham. He had made a
작은 토지를 사셨어요 호셤 근처에 있는 서섹스에.

very considerable fortune / in the States, / and his reason
큰아버지는 상당한 재산을 모으셨는데 미국에서, 그곳을 떠난 이유는

for leaving them / was his aversion to the negroes, / and
혹인에 대한 증오와,

his dislike of the Republican policy / in extending the
공화당 정책에 대한 반감 때문이었죠 혹인에게도 선거권을 허용한.

franchise to them. He was a singular man, / fierce and
큰아버지는 특이한 사람인데다,

quick-tempered, / very foul-mouthed / when he was
성격이 사납고 다혈질이며, 입이 거칠고 화가 나면,

angry, / and of a most retiring disposition. During all the
내성적인 성격이었어요. 호셤에 사는 동안 내내,

years that he lived at Horsham, / I doubt if ever he set
읍내에 발을 들여놓은 적은 있는지

foot in the town.
의심스러울 정도예요.

He had a garden and two or three fields / round his
정원과 밭 두세 곳을 가지고 계셨는데 집 주변에,

house, / and there he would take his exercise, / though
그곳에서 운동을 하시곤 했죠,

very often / for weeks on end / he would never leave his
하지만 자주 몇 주 동안은 방 밖으로 나가지 않곤 했어요.

room. He drank a great deal of brandy / and smoked very
술을 많이 마시고 담배도 많이 피우셨지만,

heavily, / but he would see no society / and did not want
사람들과의 교제가 전혀 없었고, 친구 사귀기도 싫어하셨죠,

any friends, / not even his own brother.
심지어 형제조차도.

---

estate 토지 | aversion 아주 싫어함, 혐오감 | negroes (모욕적) 혹인 | franchise 선거권 | singular 특이한 |
quick-tempered 화를 잘 내는 | foul-mouthed 입버릇이 상스러운 | retiring 내성적인 | disposition 성격

He didn't mind me; / in fact, / he took a fancy to me, /
저를 싫어하진 않으셨어요;   사실,   저를 예뻐하셨죠,

for at the time when he saw me first / I was a youngster
저를 처음 보았을 때   제가 열두 살쯤이었거든요.

of twelve or so. This would be in the year 1878, / after he
그게 1878년의 일이었는데,

had been eight or nine years in England. He begged my
영국에서 지내신 지 8, 9년쯤 되었을 때였죠.   아버지께 부탁하셨죠

father / to let me live with him / and he was very kind
저를 데리고 살게 해 달라고   친절하게 대해 주셨어요

to me / in his way. When he was sober / he used to be
나름대로.   술에 취하지 않을 때는

fond of playing / backgammon and draughts / with me, /
노는 것을 좋아하셨고   주사위 놀이나 체커 게임을 하면서   저와,

and he would make me his representative / both with the
저를 대리인으로 내세우셨어요

servants and with the tradespeople, / so that by the time
하인이나 상인들을 대할 때,   그래서 열여섯 살이 되었을 때

that I was sixteen / I was quite master of the house.
저는 집안의 주인이나 다름없었죠.

I kept all the keys / and could go where I liked / and do
모든 열쇠를 보관하고   가고 싶은 곳은 어디든지 가고   하고 싶은

what I liked, / so long as I did not disturb him in his
일도 할 수 있었죠,   큰아버지의 사생활을 방해하지만 않는다면.

privacy. There was one singular exception, / however,
한 가지 예외가 있었는데,   하지만,

/ for he had a single room, / a lumber-room up / among
방이 하나 있었고   헛간으로 쓰이는

the attics, / which was invariably locked, / and which he
다락방 중에서,   그곳은 항상 잠겨 있었고,

would never permit / either me or anyone else to enter.
절대 허락하지 않으셨어요   저나 다른 누군가가 들어가는 것을.

---

backgammon (두 사람이 하는) 주사위 놀이 | draughts 체커 게임(보드 게임의 일종)(=checkers) |
representative 대리인 | tradespeople 자영업자들, 장인(匠人)들 | lumber-room 헛간 | attic 다락 |
invariably 언제나

With a boy's curiosity / I have peeped / through the
소년의 호기심으로　　　　　　　엿보기도 했지만

keyhole, / but I was never able to see / more than such
열쇠 구멍으로,　 하지만 전혀 보이지 않았어요

a collection of old trunks and bundles / as would be
낡은 트렁크와 짐 꾸러미 외에는

expected in such a room.
그런 방이면 있을 법한.

One day / — it was in March, 1883 — / a letter with
어느 날　　　— 1883년 3월이었는데 —　　　　외국 우표가 붙은 편지

a foreign stamp / lay upon the table / in front of the
한 통이　　　　　탁자 위에 놓여 있었죠

colonel's plate. It was not a common thing / for him
대령 명패 앞에.　　흔한 일이 아니었어요　　　　　　큰아버지가

to receive letters, / for his bills were all paid in ready
우편물을 받는 일은,　　　청구서는 모두 미리 지불했고,

money, / and he had no friends of any sort.
　　　　　친구도 없었으니까요.

Key Expression

so long as ~ : ~ 하는 한
so long as~는 '~하는 동안', 또는 '~하는 한'의 두 가지 의미를 가지고 있습니다. so 대신에 as를 사용해도 같은 의미가 됩니다.

ex) I kept all the keys and could go where I liked and do what I liked, so long as I did not disturb him in his privacy.
큰아버지의 사생활을 방해하지 않는 한, 제가 모든 열쇠를 보관했고 가고 싶은 곳은 어디든지 갈 수 있었어요.

---

* 인도 남동부에 있는 퐁디셰리 주의 주도. 1674년 프랑스가 지역 통치자에게 구입한 후, 프랑스 무역의 중심지 역할을 했다. 1761년 영국의 식민지가 되었다가 1954년 인도령이 되었다.

postmark (우편물의) 소인 | patter 후두두 하는 소리를 내다 | protrude 튀어나오다 | putty 퍼티(유리를 창틀에 끼울 때 바르는 접합제) | glare 노려보다 | trembling 떨리는 | palpitate 두근거리다 | scrawl 휘갈겨 쓰다 | flap 덮개

'From India!' / said he / as he took it up, / '*Pondicherry
'인도에서라고!' 말씀하셨어요 편지를 집어들며, '퐁디셰리 소인이라니!

postmark! What can this be?'
무슨 일이지?'

Opening it hurriedly, / out there / jumped five little dried
서둘러 편지를 열자, 편지 밖으로 오렌지 씨앗 다섯 개가 나오더니.

orange pips, / which pattered down upon his plate. I
명패 위로 후드득 떨어졌어요.

began to laugh at this, / but the laugh was struck from
저는 이를 보고 웃음을 터뜨렸지만, 웃음이 싹 가셨죠

my lips / at the sight of his face. His lip had fallen, / his
큰아버지의 얼굴을 보고. 큰아버지는 입을 벌린 채,

eyes were protruding, / his skin the colour of putty, /
두 눈은 뛰어나올 듯 커졌고, 얼굴은 잿빛으로 변했어요,

and he glared at the envelope / which he still held in his
큰아버지는 봉투를 뚫어져라 쳐다보더니

trembling hand, / 'K. K. K.!' / he shrieked, / and then, /
떨리는 손으로 들고 있던, 'K, K, K!' 라고 외치셨어요. 그리고 나서,

'My God, my God, / my sins have overtaken me!'
'맙소사, 제 죄값을 치르게 되었군요!'

'What is it, / uncle?' / I cried.
'그게 뭔가요, 큰아버지?' 제가 소리쳤죠.

'Death,' / said he, / and rising from the table / he retired
'죽음이다,' 말씀하시며, 탁자에서 일어나

to his room, / leaving me palpitating with horror.
방으로 들어가셨죠, 무서워서 가슴이 두근거리는 저를 남겨 두고.

I took up the envelope / and saw scrawled in red ink /
저는 봉투를 집어들고 붉은 잉크로 휘갈겨 쓴 글씨를 보았는데

upon the inner flap, / just above the gum, / the letter K
펼쳐진 봉투 안쪽에, 풀 바로 위쪽이었고, K

three times repeated. There was nothing else / save the
K자가 세 번 쓰여 있었어요. 다른 것은 없었어요

five dried pips.
다섯 개의 마른 씨앗 말고는.

What could be the reason / of his overpowering terror?
이유가 뭘까요   큰아버지가 공포에 떨었던?

I left the breakfast-table, / and as I ascended the stair / I
저는 아침 식탁을 떠나,   계단을 올라가다가

met him coming down / with an old rusty key, / which
내려오던 큰 아버지와 마주쳤는데   낡고 녹슨 열쇠를 들고,

must have belonged to the attic, / in one hand, / and a
그 다락방 열쇠가 틀림없는,   한 손에,

small brass box, / like a cashbox, / in the other.
그리고 작은 놋쇠함을,   금고처럼 생긴,   다른 손에 들고 계셨죠.

'They may do what they like, / but I'll checkmate them
'하고 싶은 대로 하라지,   하지만 나도 가만히 당하진 않을 테다,'

still,' / said he with an oath.
맹세하듯 말씀하셨어요.

'Tell Mary / that I shall want a fire in my room / to-day, /
'메리에게 일러라   내 방에 불을 때고   오늘,

and send down to Fordham, / the Horsham lawyer.'
포덤에게 가라고,   호셤의 변호사인.'

I did as he ordered, / and when the lawyer arrived / I
저는 시키는 대로 했고,   변호사가 도착하자

was asked to step up to the room. The fire was burning
방에 올라가 있으라는 말을 들었죠.   난로가 활활 타고 있었는데,

brightly, / and in the grate / there was a mass of black,
쇠살대 안에   검은 재가 있었고,

fluffy ashes, / as of burned paper, / while the brass box /
종이를 태운 듯한,   놋쇠함은

stood open and empty / beside it. As I glanced at the box
열린 채 텅 비어 있었어요   그 옆에.   놋쇠함을 흘긋 보고

/ I noticed, / with a start, / that upon the lid / was printed
알았어요,   시작 부분에,   뚜껑 위의   그 K자가 쓰여 있다

the treble K / which I had read in the morning / upon the
는 것을   아침에 읽었던

envelope.
봉투에서.

ascend 올라가다 | rusty 녹슨 | brass 놋쇠 | cashbox 돈궤, 금고 | checkmate 장군을 부르다, 궁지에 몰아넣다
| grate (난로 안의 연료를 받치는) 쇠살대 | fluffy 솜털의, 솜털로 뒤덮인

'I wish you, / John,' / said my uncle, / 'to witness my
'부탁인데, 존,' 큰아버지가 말씀하셨죠, '내 유언장의 증인이 되어

will. I leave my estate, / with all its advantages and all its
주렴. 내 토지를 물려 주겠다, 그 모든 이익과 불이익도 함께,

disadvantages, / to my brother, / your father, / whence it
내 동생인, 네 아버지에게, 그로부터 넘어갈

will, / no doubt, / descend to you. If you can enjoy it / in
거다, 물론, 네게. 네가 그것을 누릴 수 있다면

peace, / well and good! If you find you cannot, / take my
평화롭게, 좋은 일일 게야! 만약 그렇지 못하다면, 내 충고를 듣고,

advice, / my boy, / and leave it to your deadliest enemy.
애야, 그걸 네 가장 끔찍한 원수에게 넘기거라.

I am sorry to give you / such a two-edged thing, / but
물려 줘서 미안하구나 그런 양날의 칼과 같은 것을,

I can't say / what turn things are going to take. Kindly
하지만 모르겠다 일이 어떻게 돌아갈지.

sign the paper / where Mr. Fordham shows you.'
종이에 서명하거라 포덤 씨가 알려 주는 곳에.'

I signed the paper / as directed, / and the lawyer took
저는 서류에 서명했고 시키는 대로, 변호사는 그걸 가지고 갔어요.

it away with him. The singular incident made, / as you
이 특이한 사건은,

may think, / the deepest impression upon me, / and I
짐작하시다시피, 제게 깊은 인상을 주었고,

pondered over it / and turned it every way in my mind /
그 일에 대해 깊이 생각하고 마음속으로 이리저리 따져 보았지만

without being able to make anything of it. Yet / I could
아무것도 알 수 없었어요. 하지만

not shake off / the vague feeling of dread / which it left
떨쳐낼 수 없었지만 막연한 두려움을 그 일 뒤에 감춰진,

behind, / though the sensation grew less keen / as the
감정이 누그러졌지요

weeks passed / and nothing happened / to disturb the
몇 주가 지나고 아무 일도 일어나지 않자

usual routine of our lives. I could see a change in my
일상 생활을 방해할 만한. 큰아버지에게서 변화가 보였죠,

uncle, / however. He drank more than ever, / and he was
하지만.　전보다 술을 더 많이 마셨고,　더욱 꺼리셨어요

less inclined / for any sort of society. Most of his time /
어떤 종류의 만남도.　대부분의 시간을

he would spend in his room, / with the door locked upon
방 안에서 보내셨는데,　문을 걸어 잠근 채

the inside, / but sometimes / he would emerge / in a sort
가끔씩　나타나더니　술에 취한 미친

of drunken frenzy / and would burst out of the house /
사람같은 모습으로　집 밖으로 뛰어나가

and tear about the garden / with a revolver in his hand, /
정원을 누비고 다니셨어요　손에 총을 들고.

screaming out / that he was afraid of no man, / and that
고함을 지르며　아무도 두렵지 않다고,

he was not to be cooped up, / like a sheep in a pen, / by
또 자신은 갇히지 않을 거라고,　우리 안의 양처럼,

man or devil. When these hot fits were over, / however, /
사람이든 악마이든.　이런 발작이 멈추면,　하지만,

he would rush tumultuously in at the door / and lock and
요란하게 방 안으로 들어가

bar it behind him, / like a man who can brazen it out /
문을 걸어 잠그셨어요,　마치 뻔뻔하게 대항할 수 없는 사람처럼

no longer / against the terror / which lies at the roots of
더 이상　공포에 맞서　마음 깊은 곳에 자리잡고 있는.

his soul. At such times / I have seen his face, / even on a
그럴 때　큰 아버지 얼굴을 보면,　추운 날씨임에도

cold day, / glisten with moisture, / as though it were new
불구하고,　물기로 반짝였어요,　대야에서 막 얼굴을 든 것처럼.

raised from a basin.

---

whence (~한) 곳에서 | descend 내려가다 | ponder 곰곰이 생각하다 | turn~in one´s mind 가만히 생각해
보다 | dread 두려움 | sensation 느낌, 감각 | inclined (~을) 하고 싶은, (마음이) 내키는 | emerge 나오다 |
frenzy 광분, 광란 | coop up 가두다 | fit 발작 | tumultuously 시끄럽게 | brazen it out 뻔뻔하게 행동하다 |
glisten 반짝이다 | basin 대야

Well, / to come to an end of the matter, / Mr. Holmes,
자, 이야기를 마무리 짓자면, 홈즈 씨,

/ and not to abuse your patience, / there came a night
선생의 인내심을 시험하지 않기 위해, 어느 날 밤이었어요

/ when he made one of those drunken sallies / from
큰아버지는 술에 취해 갑자기 뛰어 나가더니

which he never came back. We found him, / when we
돌아오지 않으셨어요. 발견했죠,

went to search for him, / face downward / in a little
찾으러 나갔을 때, 엎어져 있는 모습을

green-scummed pool, / which lay at the foot of the
녹색 찌꺼기가 떠 있는 수영장 안에, 정원 아래에 있는.

garden. There was no sign of any violence, / and the
폭행의 흔적은 없었고,

water was but two feet deep, / so that the jury, / having
물의 깊이가 2피트 밖에 안 되었기에, 배심원은,

regard to his known eccentricity, / brought in a verdict
큰아버지의 잘 알려진 별난 행동을 고려하여, '자살' 이란 평결을 내렸어요.

of 'suicide.' But I, / who knew / how he winced / from
하지만 전, 알고 있기에 큰아버지가 움찔하던 모습을

the very thought of death, / had much ado to persuade
죽음에 대한 생각만으로도, 제 자신을 설득하기 힘들었죠

myself / that he had gone out of his way to meet it. The
큰아버지가 그런 식으로 죽음을 맞이했다고.

matter passed, / however, / and my father entered into
사건은 지나갔고, 하지만, 아버지가 토지의 소유주가 되셨어요.

possession of the estate, / and of some £14,000, / which
14,000파운드와,

lay to his credit at the bank."
은행에 예금되어 있던."

sally 기습 공격 | scum 찌꺼기, 거품 | eccentricity 별난 행동 | verdict 평결 | wince 움찔하고 놀라다 | ado
야단법석, 고생

A. 다음 문장을 해석해 보세요.

(1) In the latter, / as may be remembered, / Sherlock Holmes was able, / by winding up the dead man's watch, / to prove / that it had been wound up two hours before, / and that therefore the deceased had gone to bed / within that time.

→

(2) His reason for leaving them / was his aversion to the negroes, / and his dislike of the Republican policy / in extending the franchise to them.

→

(3) I kept all the keys / and could go where I liked / and do what I liked, / so long as I did not disturb him in his privacy.

→

(4) I was never able to see / more than such a collection of old trunks and bundles / as would be expected in such a room.

→

B. 다음 주어진 문장이 되도록 빈칸에 써서 넣으세요.

(1) 내 아는 한, 내 자신에 대한 사항은 이 끔찍한 사건과 관련이 없다.

My own affairs have, _____, little to do with this awful business.

(2) 읍내에 발을 들여놓은 적은 있는지 의심스럽다.

→

(3) 그는 저나 다른 누군가가 들어가는 것을 절대 허락하지 않는다.

He would never permit _____.

A. (1) 후자의 사건에서 셜록 홈즈는 죽은 사람의 시계 태엽을 감아서, 두 시간 전에 시계 태엽이 감겼으며 따라서 죽은 사람이 잠자리에 든 것은 두 시간 전 이내라는 사실을 밝혀내는 것이 가능했다. (2) 그분이 그곳을 떠난 이유는 흑인에 대한 증오와 흑인에게 선거권을 허용한 공화당 정책에 대한 반감 때문이었죠. (3) 저는 모든 열쇠를 보관했고 큰아버지의 사생활을 방해하지만 않는다면 가고 싶은 곳은 어디든지 가고 하고 싶은 일

(4) 그분은 대부분의 시간을 <u>문을 안에서 걸어 잠근 채</u> 방 안에서 보내셨어요.

Most of his time he would spend in his room, [_____]

[_____]

C. 다음 주어진 문구가 알맞은 문장이 되도록 순서를 맞춰 보세요.

(1) 이런 날씨와 이런 시간에 <u>사람을 밖으로 나오게 하진 않겠지.</u>
(less / out / Nothing / a man / would / bring)
[_____] on such a day and
at such an hour.

(2) 사과 드리겠습니다.
(you / I / an apology / owe)
→

(3) 하고 싶은 대로 하라지
(what / do / They / like / they / may)
→

(4) 그분은 저와 같이 살게 해 달라고 아버지께 부탁했어요.
(live / He / me / with / my father / let / begged / him / to)
→

D. 다음 단어에 대한 맞는 설명과 연결해 보세요.

(1) peculiar   ▶   ◀ ① stick out

(2) surmise   ▶   ◀ ② great excitement

(3) protrude   ▶   ◀ ③ strange or unusual

(4) frenzy   ▶   ◀ ④ uncertain guess

"One moment," / Holmes interposed, / "your statement
"잠깐만요," 홈즈가 끼어들었다, "당신 이야기는,

is, / I foresee, / one of the most remarkable / to which I
내가 짐작컨대, 가장 놀랄 만한 이야기 중 하나로군요

have ever listened. Let me have the date of the reception
지금껏 들었던. 날짜를 알려 주시오

/ by your uncle of the letter, / and the date of his
큰아버지가 편지를 받은, 그리고 자살한 날로 추정되는 날짜도."

supposed suicide."

"The letter arrived / on March 10, 1883. His death was /
"편지는 도착했어요 1883년 3월 10일에. 돌아가신 건

seven weeks later, / upon the night of May 2nd."
7주 후인, 5월 2일 밤이었고요."

"Thank you. Pray proceed."
"감사합니다. 계속하세요."

"When my father took over / the Horsham property, / he,
"아버지가 상속 받으셨을 때 호셤의 별장을, 아버지는,

/ at my request, / made a careful examination of the attic,
제 부탁으로, 다락방을 자세히 살펴보셨어요,

/ which had been always locked up. We found the brass
항상 잠겨 있던. 그곳에서 놋쇠함을 발견했죠,

box there, / although its contents had been destroyed.
내용물은 망가져 버렸지만요.

On the inside of the cover / was a paper label, / with
뚜껑 안쪽에 종이 라벨이 붙어 있었는데,

the initials of K. K. K. repeated upon it, / and 'Letters,
그 위에 K.K.K.라는 이니셜이 써 있고,

memoranda, receipts, and a register' / written beneath.
그리고 '편지, 메모, 영수증, 명단'이라고 그 밑에 쓰여 있었어요.

---

interpose 끼어들다 I foresee 예견하다 I pray 제발, ~해 주세요(=please) I presume 추정하다 I repute 평판,
명성 I carpet-bag 여행용 가방

These, / we presume, / indicated the nature of the papers
이것은, 우리가 추정하기에, 종이의 성격을 나타내는 것 같았어요

/ which had been destroyed / by Colonel Openshaw. For
불태워 버린 큰아버지가.

the rest, / there was nothing of much importance / in the
그 밖에는, 그다지 중요한 것이 없었어요 다락방에는

attic / save a great many scattered papers and / note-
널려 있는 수많은 신문과 공책 외에는

books / bearing upon my uncle's life / in America. Some
큰아버지의 삶을 기록한 미국에서의.

of them were of the war time / and showed / that he had
그 일부는 전쟁에 관한 것으로 기록되어 있었죠 큰아버지가 임무를

done his duty well / and had borne the repute of a brave
잘 완수했으며 용감한 군인으로서 명성을 얻었다고.

soldier. Others were / of a date during the reconstruction
다른 공책은 남부 재건 시기에 관한 것이었는데,

of the Southern states, / and were mostly concerned with
대부분 정치와 관련된 내용이었어요,

politics, / for he had evidently / taken a strong part / in
그러니 큰아버지는 분명히 열렬히 참여하신 게 틀림없어요

opposing the carpet-bag politicians / who had been sent
뜨내기 정치인을 반대하는 일에 북부에서 파견되어 내려온.

down from the North.

Key Expression

부사구 도치

장소나 방향의 부사 혹은 부사구가 문장 맨 앞에 나왔을 때, 뒤따르는 주어와 동사의 위치가 바뀌는 도치가 일어납니다.

단 동사를 수식하는 부사일 때, 자동사가 쓰인 경우에만 도치가 일어나며, 부사구 뒤에 콤마가 쓰이거나 주어가 대명사일 경우에는 도치가 일어나지 않습니다.

ex) On the inside of the cover was a paper label, with the initials of K. K. K. repeated upon it.
뚜껑 안쪽에 K.K.K.라는 이니셜이 쓰여진 종이 라벨이 붙어 있었다.
So perfect was the organisation of the society, and so systematic its methods, that there is hardly a case upon record
모임의 조직이 매우 완벽했고, 방법이 매우 체계적이어서, 기록된 사건이 거의 없다.

Well, / it was the beginning of '84 / when my father came
음, 1884년 초였어요 아버지가 호섬에 와서 살기 시작한

to live at Horsham, / and all went as well as possible with
것은, 그리고 모든 일은 더할 나위 없이 좋았죠

us / until the January of '85. On the fourth day after the
1885년 1월까지는. 1885년 1월 4일에

new year / I heard my father give a sharp cry of surprise
아버지가 놀라서 날카로운 비명을 지르시는 것이 들렸어요

/ as we sat together at the breakfast-table. There he was, /
아침 식탁에 같이 앉아 있을 때. 거기에서 아버지는,

sitting / with a newly opened envelope / in one hand / and
앉아 계셨죠 막 개봉한 봉투를 들고 한 손에는

five dried orange pips / in the outstretched palm of the
다섯 개의 오렌지 씨앗을 든 채 쭉 뻗은 다른 손바닥에는.

other one. He had always laughed / at what he called my
아버지는 항상 비웃으셨거든요 터무니없는 이야기라고 부르며

cock-and-bull story / about the colonel, / but he looked
큰아버지 이야기에 대해,

very scared and puzzled / now that the same thing had
하지만 매우 놀라고 당황하신 듯 보였죠 똑같은 일이 자신에게 일어났으니까.

come upon himself.

'Why, / what on earth does this mean, / John?' / he
'흠, 도대체 이게 뭐지, 존?'

stammered.
아버지가 말을 더듬었어요.

My heart had turned to lead.
제 심장은 뛰기 시작했죠.

'It is K. K. K.,' / said I.
'K. K. K.예요,' 제가 말했어요.

He looked inside the envelope.
아버지는 봉투 안쪽을 살펴보았어요.

'So it is,' / he cried.
'그렇구나,' 아버지가 말했죠.

---

cock-and-bull 엉뚱한, 엉터리인 | sundial 해시계 | grip 꽉 잡다 | tomfoolery 바보 같은 짓 | preposterous
말도 안 되는 | nothing of the sort (강한 부정) 그런 일은 안 한다, 당치도 않다

'Here are the very letters. But what is this / written
'여기 같은 글자가 있구나,   하지만 이건 뭐지

above them?'
그 위에 씌어 있는?'

'Put the papers on the sundial,' / I read, / peeping over
'서류를 해시계 위에 놓으시오,'   제가 읽었죠, 아버지 어깨 너머로.

his shoulder.

'What papers? What sundial?' / he asked.
'무슨 서류?   무슨 해시계?'   아버지가 물었어요.

'The sundial in the garden. There is no other,' / said I; /
'해시계는 정원에 있어요.   다른 건 없어요.'   제가 말했죠;

'but the papers must be those that are destroyed.'
'하지만 서류는 불태운 것을 말하는 게 틀림없어요.'

'Pooh!' / said he, / gripping hard at his courage.
'저런!'   아버지가 말했죠, 마음을 다잡으며.

'We are in a civilised land here, / and we can't have
'우리는 문명 국가에 살고 있는데,   이런 바보 같은 일은 있을 수 없어.

tomfoolery of this kind. Where does the thing come
어디에서 온 거니?'

from?'

'From Dundee,' / I answered, / glancing at the postmark.
'던디에서요,'   제가 대답했어요, 소인을 보고.

'Some preposterous practical joke,' / said he.
'말도 안 되는 장난이구나,'   아버지가 말씀하셨죠.

'What have I to do / with sundials and papers? I shall
'내가 무슨 상관이 있어   해시계나 서류랑?   신경 쓰지 않을

take / no notice of such nonsense.'
테다   그런 말도 안 되는 일엔.'

'I should certainly speak to the police,' / I said.
'경찰에 신고해야겠어요,'   제가 말했어요.

'And be laughed at for my pains. Nothing of the sort.'
'그러면 웃음거리가 될 거다.   그렇겐 못하지.'

'Then let me do so?'
'그럼 제가 할까요?'

'No, / I forbid you. I won't have a fuss made / about such
'아니다. 하지 말거라.   소란은 피우지 않겠다   이런 말도 안 되는

nonsense.'
일로.'

It was in vain / to argue with him, / for he was a very
소용없었어요   아버지와 말다툼하는 건,   아주 완고한 분이시니까요.

obstinate man. I went about, / however, / with a heart
저는 지내면서,   하지만,

which was full of forebodings.
불길한 예감에 사로잡혀 있었어요.

On the third day / after the coming of the letter / my
사흘 째 되던 날   편지가 도착한 지

father went from home / to visit an old friend of his,
아버지가 집을 떠나셨어요   옛 친구인 프리보디 소령을 만나러,

Major Freebody, / who is in command / of one of the
소령은 통솔하는 분이셨죠

forts upon Portsdown Hill. I was glad that he should go,
포츠다운 언덕의 요새 중 한 곳을.   저는 아버지가 가시는 걸 반겼어요,

/ for it seemed to me / that he was farther from danger /
그건 마치   아버지가 위험에서 멀어지는 듯 했으니까요

when he was away from home. In that, / however, / I was
집에서 멀리 떠나 계시면.   그것이,   하지만,

in error. Upon the second day of his absence / I received
제 실수였어요. 집을 비우신 후 이틀째 되던 날

a telegram from the major, / imploring me to come at
소령에게 전보를 받았어요,   제게 바로 오라고 요청하는.

once.
once.

My father had fallen over / one of the deep chalk-pits
아버지가 떨어져서　　　　　　　깊은 백악갱 속으로

/ which abound in the neighbourhood, / and was lying
주변에 많이 있던,　　　　　　　　　의식을 잃고 누워 계시다는

senseless, / with a shattered skull. I hurried to him, /
거예요,　　두개골이 부서진 채.　　　저는 서둘러 갔지만,

but he passed away / without having ever recovered his
아버지는 돌아가셨어요　　의식을 회복하지 못한 채.

consciousness. He had, / as it appears, / been returning
아버지는,　　아마도,　　페어럼으로부터 돌아오는

from Fareham / in the twilight, / and as the country was
중인 듯 했는데　해질 무렵에,　그 마을이 낯선 데다,

unknown to him, / and the chalk-pit unfenced, / the jury
백악갱에 울타리가 없어서,

had no hesitation / in bringing in a verdict / of 'death
배심원들은 주저하지 않고　평결을 내렸어요

from accidental causes.' Carefully as I examined / every
'사고사' 라고.　　자세히 조사했지만

fact connected with his death, / I was unable to find
아버지의 죽음과 관련된 모든 사항을,　알아낼 수 없었어요

anything / which could suggest the idea of murder. There
타살을 암시하는 듯한 단서를.

were no signs of violence, / no footmarks, no robbery, /
폭행의 흔적도 없었고,　　발자국도, 도난도 없었으며,

no record of strangers having been seen / upon the roads.
낯선 이를 목격했다는 기록도 없었어요　그 길에서.

And yet / I need not tell you / that my mind was far from
하지만　말할 필요도 없이　제 마음은 전혀 편치 않았고,

at ease, / and that I was well-nigh certain / that some foul
거의 확신하고 있어요　어떤 사악한 음모가

plot / had been woven round him.
아버지 주위에 있었다는 것을.

---

fuss 호들갑 | in vain 헛되이 | obstinate 고집 센 | foreboding (불길한) 예감 | telegram 전보 | implore
간청하다 | chalk-pits (석회석를 채취하는) 백악갱 | shattered 산산이 부서진 | skull 두개골 | consciousness
의식 | verdict 평결 | well-nigh 거의

In this sinister way / I came into my inheritance. You
이런 불길한 방식으로　　　저는 유산을 상속 받았어요.

will ask me / why I did not dispose of it? I answer, /
물으시겠죠　　왜 그 재산을 처분하지 않는지?　　대답하자면,

because I was well convinced / that our troubles were /
확신하고 있기 때문이에요　　　우리 집 문제는

in some way / dependent upon an incident in my uncle's
어떤 면에서　　큰아버지의 삶 속의 어떤 사건과 관계가 있기 때문에,

life, / and that the danger would be as pressing / in one
위험은 마찬가지일 거라고　　　우리 집에서나

house / as in another.
다른 집에 가서나.

It was in January, '85, / that my poor father met his end,
1885년 1월이었어요,　　가여운 아버지가 돌아가신 것이,

/ and two years and eight months have elapsed / since
그리고 2년 8개월이 흘렀죠　　　그 이후로,

then. During that time / I have lived happily at Horsham,
그 동안　　　저는 호셤에서 행복하게 살았어요,

/ and I had begun to hope / that this curse had passed
희망을 갖기 시작했죠　　　이 저주가 사라졌을 거라고

away / from the family, / and that it had ended / with the
우리 가족에게서,　　　그리고 끝났다고

last generation. I had begun to take comfort / too soon, /
아버지 세대에서.　　저는 안정을 찾기 시작한 거예요　　너무 빨리,

however; / yesterday morning / the blow fell / in the very
하지만;　　어제 아침　　　그 충격이 다가왔죠　　같은 모습으로

shape / in which it had come upon my father."
아버지에게 일어났던 것과."

---

sinister 불길한 | inheritance 유산 | dispose of 처리하다 | pressing 거절하기 힘든 | elapse (시간이) 흐르다
| curse 욕(설), 악담

The young man took from his waistcoat / a crumpled
젊은이는 조끼에서 꺼내어 구겨진 봉투를,

envelope, / and turning to the table / he shook out / upon
탁자 위로 가져오더니 흔들어 떨어뜨렸다 탁자 위에

it / five little dried orange pips.
다섯 개의 오렌지 씨앗을.

"This is the envelope," / he continued.
"이것이 그 봉투예요," 그가 계속 말했다.

"The postmark is London / — eastern division. Within
"런던 소인이에요 — 동쪽 지구요.

are the very words / which were upon my father's last
안에는 그 단어가 있고요 아버지가 마지막 남긴 말인:

message: / 'K. K. K.'; / and then 'Put the papers on the
'K. K. K' 요; 그리고 '서류를 해시계 위에 올려 놓으시오' 라고."

sundial.'"

"What have you done?" / asked Holmes.
"어떻게 했소?" 홈즈가 물었다.

"Nothing."
"아무 일도."

"Nothing?"
"아무 일도?"

"To tell the truth" / — he sank his face into his thin,
"솔직히 말하면" — 그는 마르고 창백한 손으로 얼굴을 감쌌다 —

white hands — / "I have felt helpless. I have felt like
"감당할 수 없어요. 불쌍한 토끼가 된 기분이에요

one of those poor rabbits / when the snake is writhing
뱀이 몸부림치며 다가오는 앞에 선.

towards it. I seem to be in the grasp / of some resistless,
사로잡힌 것 같아요 저항할 수 없고, 거침없는 악당

inexorable evil, / which no foresight and no precautions
에게, 예견하고 조심해도 맞서서 지킬 수 없는."

can guard against."

---

crumpled 구겨진 | helpless 무력한, 감당하지 못하는 | writhe 몸부림치다 | resistless 저항할 수 없는 |
inexorable 거침없는 | tut 쯧 | clench 꽉 쥐다 | imbecility 바보짓, 어리석은 말

"Tut! Tut!" / cried Sherlock Holmes.
쯧! 쯧!" 홈즈가 소리쳤다.

"You must act, man, / or you are lost. Nothing but
"행동해야 해요, 아니면 죽을 거요.

energy can save you. This is no time for despair."
힘을 내야만 살아날 수 있소. 절망에 빠져 있을 시간이 없어요."

"I have seen the police."
"경찰에 갔었어요."

"Ah!"
"아!"

"But they listened to my story with a smile. I am
"하지만 제 이야기를 듣고 웃더군요.

convinced / that the inspector has formed the opinion
분명히 경찰은 생각하는 것 같았어요

/ that the letters are all practical jokes, / and that the
편지는 모두 장난이고,

deaths of my relations were really accidents, / as the
친척들의 죽음은 사고였다고, 배심원이

jury stated, / and were not to be connected / with the
평결했듯이, 관계가 없다고요

warnings."
그 편지의 경고와는."

Holmes shook his clenched hands / in the air.
홈즈는 꼭 쥔 주먹을 휘둘렀다 공중에.

"Incredible imbecility!" / he cried.
"정말 멍청하군!" 그가 소리쳤다.

"They have, / however, / allowed me a policeman, / who
"그들은, 하지만, 경찰관 한 명을 보내 주었어요,

may remain in the house with me."
제 집에서 저와 함께 머무르도록."

"Has he come with you to-night?"
"오늘 밤 같이 왔나요?"

"No. His orders were / to stay in the house."
"아뇨. 그가 받은 명령은 집에 있으라는 것이니까요."

Again / Holmes raved in the air.
다시 한 번 홈즈는 허공에 대고 소리를 질렀다.

"Why did you come to me," / he cried, / "and, / above
"왜 나를 찾아왔소," 그가 소리쳤다. "그리고, 무엇보다,

all, / why did you not come at once?"
왜 즉시 찾아오지 않았소?"

"I did not know. It was only to-day / that I spoke to
"몰랐어요. 오늘에서야 프렌더개스트 소령님께

Major Prendergast / about my troubles / and was advised
말씀 드렸고 제 문제에 대해 충고를 들었죠

by him / to come to you."
당신을 찾아가 보라고."

"It is really two days / since you had the letter. We
"정말 이틀이나 되었나 편지를 받은 후로.

should have acted before this. You have no further
그 전에 움직였어야 했는데. 더 이상 증거는 없겠군,

evidence, / I suppose, / than that which you have placed
내 생각에, 우리 앞에 내놓은 것 외에

before us / — no suggestive detail which might help us?"
— 도움이 될 만한 사항이 없소?"

"There is one thing," / said John Openshaw.
"하나 있어요." 존이 말했다.

He rummaged in his coat pocket, / and, / drawing out a
그는 외투 주머니를 뒤지더니, 그리고, 종이 조각을 꺼내어

piece / of discoloured, blue-tinted paper, / he laid it out
변색되고 푸른빛을 띠는, 탁자 위에 올려 놓았다.

upon the table.

---

raye (화가 나서) 미친 듯이 악을 쓰다 | rummage 뒤지다 | discoloured 변색된 | flutter 펄럭이다 | ragged
들쑥날쑥한 | enigmatical 수수께끼 같은

"I have some remembrance," / said he, / "that on the day
"기억이 나요."
그가 말했다.

when my uncle burned the papers / I observed / that the
"큰아버지가 종이를 태운 그날
보았어요

small, unburned margins / which lay amid the ashes /
타지 않은 작은 종이 조각이
재 속에 있던

were of this particular colour. I found this single sheet /
이 독특한 색깔이었죠.
이 조각을 발견했는데

upon the floor of his room, / and I am inclined to think
큰아버지 방바닥에서,
생각이 들었죠

/ that it may be one of the papers / which has, / perhaps,
이게 그 서류의 일부분이라고
그건,
아마도,

/ fluttered out from among the others, / and in that way
서류에서 떨어져 나와서,
이런 식으로

/ has escaped destruction. Beyond the mention of pips,
타지 않고 남은 거겠죠.
씨앗에 대한 이야기 외에,

/ I do not see / that it helps us much. I think myself /
모르겠지만요
도움이 될지.
제 생각에

that it is a page from some private diary. The writing is
이건 일기의 한 부분 같아요.

undoubtedly my uncle's."
틀림없이 큰아버지의 글씨체예요."

Holmes moved the lamp, / and we both bent over the
홈즈는 램프를 옮겼고,
우리는 몸을 굽혀 종이를 보았다.

sheet of paper, / which showed by its ragged edge / that
가장자리가 들쑥날쑥한 것을 보니

it had indeed been torn from a book. It was headed,
정말 책에서 찢겨진 조각이었다.
제목은,

/ "March, 1869," / and beneath / were the following
"1869년 3월" 이었고,
그 밑에
수수께끼 같은 글이 쓰여 있었다:

enigmatical notices:

4th. Hudson came. Same old *platform*.
4일. 허드슨 도착.   예전과 같은 행동강령.

7th. Set the pips / on McCauley, Paramore, / and John
7일. 씨앗을 보내다   맥컬리, 패러모어,

Swain, of St Augustine.
세인트 오거스틴의 존 스웨인에게.

9th. McCauley cleared.
9일. 맥컬리 제거

10th. John Swain cleared.
10일. 존 스웨인 제거

12th. Visited Paramore. All well.
12일. 패러모어 방문.   모두 해결.

"Thank you!" / said Holmes, / folding up the paper / and
"고맙소!"   홈즈가 말했다,   종이를 접어

returning it to our visitor.
방문객에게 돌려 주며.

"And now you must on no account / lose another instant.
"이제 어떤 이유로든　시간을 지체해선 안 되요.

We cannot spare time / even to discuss / what you have
시간이 없어요　이야기 할 시간조차　당신이 한 얘기에 대해.

told me. You must get home instantly and act."
즉시 집으로 가서 행동해야 합니다."

"What shall I do?"
"뭘 해야 하죠?"

"There is but one thing to do. It must be done at once.
"할 일은 한 가지밖에 없소.　즉시 해야 해요.

You must put this piece of paper / which you have shown
이 종이 조각을 넣으시오　우리에게 보여 준

us / into the brass box / which you have described. You
놋쇠함 안에　당신이 설명한.

must also put in a note / to say that all the other papers
쪽지도 넣어야 합니다　다른 서류는 모두 불태웠고

were burned / by your uncle, / and that this is the only
큰아버지가,　이게 남아 있는 유일한 것이라고 적어서.

one which remains. You must assert / that in such words
주장해야 해요

as will carry conviction with them. Having done this, /
그들에게 믿음을 줄 수 있는 말로.　이렇게 한 다음,

you must at once put the box out / upon the sundial, / as
즉시 박스를 올려 놓으시오　해시계 위에,

directed. Do you understand?"
지시한 대로.　이해하겠소?"

"Entirely."
"잘 알겠습니다."

platform 공약, 강령 | on no account 무슨 일이 있어도, 무슨 이유로든 | instantly 즉시 | assert 주장하다 |
conviction 유죄 선고

"Do not think of revenge, / or anything of the sort, / at
복수는 생각도 마시오, 그 비슷한 것도,

present. I think / that we may gain that / by means of the
당장은. 내 생각에 복수할 수 있을 거요 법에 의해;

law; / but we have our web to weave, / while theirs is
하지만 우리는 그물을 쳐야 합니다, 그들은 이미 그물을 쳐

already woven. The first consideration is / to remove the
놓았을 테니. 먼저 생각할 일은 다가오는 위험을 없애는

pressing danger / which threatens you. The second is / to
것입니다 당신을 위협하는. 두 번째는

clear up the mystery / and to punish the guilty parties."
수수께끼를 해결하고 범죄자들을 처벌하는 일이지요."

"I thank you," / said the young man, / rising and pulling
"감사합니다." 젊은이가 말했다, 일어서서 외투를 집어 들며.

on his overcoat.

"You have given me fresh life and hope. I shall certainly
"제게 새로운 활력과 희망을 주셨습니다. 꼭 하겠습니다

do / as you advise."
충고하신 대로."

"Do not lose an instant. And, / above all, / take care of
"지체하지 마세요. 그리고, 무엇보다, 조심하시오

yourself / in the meanwhile, / for I do not think that there
당분간, 의심할 여지가 없는 것 같으니까

can be a doubt / that you are threatened / by a very real
당신이 위협받고 있다는 사실이 실제로 임박한 위험에.

and imminent danger. How do you go back?"
어떻게 돌아갈 거요?"

"By train from Waterloo."
"워털루 역에서 기차를 탈 거예요."

"It is not yet nine. The streets will be crowded, / so I
"아직 9시가 안 됐군. 거리는 붐빌 테니,

trust that you may be in safety. And yet / you cannot
안전할 것 같군요. 그래도

guard yourself too closely."
각별히 조심하시오."

"I am armed."
"총을 갖고 있어요."

"That is well. To-morrow / I shall set to work upon your
"잘 됐군요.   내일   당신 사건에 대한 조사를 착수하겠소."

case."

"I shall see you at Horsham, / then?"
"호섬에서 뵐까요,   그럼?"

"No, / your secret lies in London. It is there / that I shall
"아니,   비밀은 런던에 있소.   그곳이오

seek it."
단서를 찾을 곳은."

"Then / I shall call upon you / in a day, or in two days, /
"그러면   찾아오겠습니다   하루나 이틀 후에,

with news as to the box and the papers. I shall take your
상자와 서류에 대한 소식을 가지고.   충고에 따르겠습니다

advice / in every particular."
모든 점을."

He shook hands with us / and took his leave. Outside
그는 우리와 악수를 한 후   떠났다.   밖에는

/ the wind still screamed / and the rain splashed / and
여전히 바람이 울부짖고   빗줄기가 튀며

pattered against the windows. This strange, wild story
창문을 두드리고 있었다.   이 기이하고 터무니없는 이야기는

/ seemed to have come to us / from amid the mad
우리에게 찾아온 듯 했다   사나운 자연으로부터

elements / — blown in upon us / like a sheet of sea-weed
— 우리에게 불어왔다가   강풍에 실린 해초처럼 —

in a gale — / and now to have been reabsorbed / by them
이제 다시 빨려 들어간 것 같았다   자연으로

/ once more.
다시 한 번.

imminent 임박한 | wild 무모한, 터무니없는

57

Sherlock Holmes sat / for some time / in silence, / with
셜록 홈즈는 앉아 있었다   잠시 동안   말 없이,

his head sunk forward / and his eyes bent upon the red
고개를 숙이고   활활 타오르는 벽난로 불빛로 불빛을 굽어보며.

glow of the fire. Then he lit his pipe, / and leaning back
그리고 나서 파이프 담배에 불을 붙이고,

in his chair / he watched the blue smoke-rings / as they
의자에 몸을 기댄 채   고리 모양의 푸른 연기를 바라보았다

chased each other up to the ceiling.
서로 쫓듯이 천장으로 올라가는.

"I think, / Watson," / he remarked at last, / "that of all
"내 생각엔,   왓슨,"   그가 마침내 입을 열었다,   "우리가 다룬 모든

our cases / we have had none more fantastic than this."
사건 중에   이보다 더 이상한 사건은 없었던 것 같군."

"Save, / perhaps, / the Sign of Four."
"예외겠지,   아마,   '네 사람의 서명' 사건은."

"Well, yes. Save, / perhaps, / that. And yet / this John
"음, 그렇군.   예외지,   아마,   그 사건은. 하지만

Openshaw seems to me / to be walking amid even
존 오픈쇼는 보이는 군   더한 위험에 빠질 것처럼

greater perils / than did the Sholtos."
솔토 형제보다."

"But have you," / I asked, / "formed any definite
"하지만 자네는,"   내가 물었다,   "확실히 이해했겠지

conception / as to what these perils are?"
그 위험이 무엇인지에 대해?"

"There can be no question / as to their nature," / he
"의문의 여지가 없네   위험의 성격에 대해서는,"

answered.
그가 대답했다.

"Then what are they? Who is this K. K. K., / and why
"그럼 그게 뭔가?   K. K. K.는 누구이며,

does he pursue this unhappy family?"
왜 이 불행한 가족을 쫓는 거지?"

conception 개념, 이해 | perils 위험

Sherlock Holmes closed his eyes / and placed his elbows /
셜록 홈즈는 눈을 감고 / 팔꿈치를 올려 놓더니

upon the arms of his chair, / with his finger-tips together.
의자 팔걸이에, / 손끝을 마주 잡았다.

"The ideal reasoner," / he remarked, / "would, / when he
"이상적인 추론가는," / 그가 말했다, / "하겠지,

had once been shown a single fact / in all its bearings, /
일단 한 가지 사실에 마주했을 때 / 관련된 모든 사항에서,

deduce from it / not only all the chain of events / which
추론해 내지 / 사건의 일련의 과정 뿐만 아니라

led up to it / but also all the results / which would follow
그 사실에 이르는 / 모든 결과도 / 그 사실에 뒤따르는.

from it. As *Cuvier could correctly describe / a whole
퀴비에는 정확하게 묘사할 수 있네 / 동물의 전체 모습을

animal / by the contemplation of a single bone, / so the
뼈 한 조각만 보고도, / 그래서 관찰자

observer / who has thoroughly understood one link / in
라면 / 하나의 연결 고리를 완전히 이해한

a series of incidents / should be able to accurately state
일련의 사건에서 / 정확하게 말할 수 있는 것이지

/ all the other ones, / both before and after. We have not
다른 연결 고리도, / 그 전이나 후의.

yet grasped the results / which the reason alone can attain
우리는 아직 결과를 파악하지 못했네 / 추리만으로 도달할 수 있는.

to. Problems may be solved / in the study / which have
문제는 해결될 수 있네 / 연구를 통해 / 그 연구는 당황하게

baffled / all those who have sought a solution / by the aid
만들지 / 해결책을 찾는 모든 이들을

of their senses. To carry the art, / however, / to its highest
감각에 도움을 받아. / 이 기술을 가지려면, / 그러나, / 최대한으로,

pitch, / it is necessary / that the reasoner should be able to
필요하네 / 추론가가 사용할 수 있어야 하지

utilise / all the facts / which have come to his knowledge;
모든 사실을 / 알게 된;

* 조르주 퀴비에 남작. 18세기 말~19세기 초의 프랑스 동물학자로 동물분류를 체계적으로 척추동
물, 관절동물, 연체동물, 방사동물의 4군으로 나누고 화석을 연구하여 고생물학의 기초를 닦았다.

/ and this in itself implies, / as you will readily see, /
그리고 이것은 본질적으로 의미하네,   자네도 알겠지만,

a possession of all knowledge, / which, / even in these
모든 지식을 가지고 있어야 함을,   그것은,   요즘같은 시대에도

days / of free education and encyclopaedias, / is a
    자유롭게 교육 받고 백과사전을 이용할 수 있는,

somewhat rare accomplishment. It is not so impossible,
상당히 해 내기 힘든 일이지.   불가능한 것은 아니야,

/ however, / that a man should possess all knowledge /
    그렇지만,   한 사람이 모든 지식을 알고 있는 것은,

which is likely to be useful to him / in his work, / and
유용하게 쓰일 만한   일하는 데 있어,   그리고

this / I have endeavoured in my case to do. If I remember
이것을   나는 할 수 있도록 노력해 왔네.   내가 정확히 기억한다면,

rightly, / you on one occasion, / in the early days of
    자네도 한 번,   우리의 우정이 시작된 지 얼마 안 됐을 때,

our friendship, / defined my limits / in a very precise
              내 지식의 한계를 밝혀 냈었는데 아주 정확한 방법으로."

fashion."

Key Expression ❢

with를 사용한 부대상황

두 가지 일이 동시에 일어날 때를 부대상황이라고 합니다.
with를 사용해 이를 간단하게 표현할 수 있는데, '~를 ~한 채로' 혹은 '~을
...하면서' 라고 해석합니다.

▶ with + 목적어 + 형용사[전치사구/현재분사/과거분사]

ex) Sherlock Holmes sat for some time in silence, with his head sunk forward and
his eyes bent upon the red glow of the fire.
셜록 홈즈는 고개를 숙이고 활활 타오르는 벽난로 불빛을 굽어보며 잠시 동안
말 없이 앉아 있었다
Sherlock Holmes closed his eyes and placed his elbows upon the arms of
his chair, with his finger-tips together.
셜록 홈즈는 손끝을 마주 잡은 채 눈을 감고 의자 팔걸이에 팔꿈치를 올려 놓았다.

bearings 관련, 방향 | deduce 추론하다 | contemplation 사색, 응시 | incident 사건 | attain 이루다, 이르다
| utilise 활용하다(=utilize) | in itself 본질적으로 | encyclopaedia 백과사전(=encyclopedia) | endeavour 힘껏
노력하다

"Yes," / I answered, / laughing.
"그랬지," 내가 대답했다, 웃으며.

"It was a singular document. Philosophy, astronomy,
"독특한 기록이었지. 철학, 천문학, 정치학은

and politics / were marked at zero, / I remember. Botany
0점을 기록했어, 내 기억에. 식물학은

variable, / geology profound / as regards the mud-stains /
변수가 심했고, 지질학은 이해가 깊었지 진흙 자국으로 알아낼 만큼

from any region / within fifty miles of town, / chemistry
어느 지역에서 온 것인지 마을의 50km 이내의, 화학은 별나게

eccentric, / anatomy unsystematic, / sensational
뛰어났고, 해부학은 체계가 없었으며,

literature and crime records unique, / violin-player, /
세계를 놀라게 한 문학 작품과 범죄 기록에선 독보적이었고, 바이올린 연주자이자,

boxer, swordsman, lawyer, / and self-poisoner by cocaine
권투선수, 검술사, 변호사이며, 그리고 코카인과 담배 중독자이지.

and tobacco. Those, / I think, / were the main points of
이상이, 내 생각에, 분석의 핵심 내용이었던 것 같군."

my analysis."

Holmes grinned / at the last item.
홈즈는 빙긋 웃었다 마지막 부분을 듣고.

"Well," / he said, / "I say now, / as I said then, / that a
"음," 그가 말했다, "이제 말하자면, 그때 말했듯이

man should keep his little brain-attic stocked / with all
사람은 뇌 속의 작은 다락방을 채워놓아야 하네

the furniture that he is likely to use, / and the rest / he
사용할 법한 모든 가구들로, 그리고 나머지는

can put away / in the lumber-room of his library, / where
보낼 수 있지 뇌 속의 서가 보관실로, 그곳에서

he can get it / if he wants it. Now, / for such a case / as
꺼낼 수 있지 원할 때. 이제, 이런 사건에는

the one which has been submitted to us / to-night, / we
우리에게 주어진 것과 같은 오늘 밤,

astronomy 천문학 | botany 식물학 | profound 심오한, 이해가 깊은 | eccentric 별난 | anatomy 해부학
| sensational 세계를 놀라게 하는 | grin 활짝 웃다 | lumber-room 헛간, 광 | muster 모으다, 발휘하다 |
presumption 추정 | provincial 지방의 | hypothesis 가설 | formidable 어마어마한

need certainly to muster / all our resources. Kindly hand
반드시 발휘해야 하네 · 모든 지식을. · 건네 주게

me down / the letter K of the 'American Encyclopaedia'
'미국 대백과사전' 의 K 부분을

/ which stands upon the shelf beside you. Thank you.
자네 옆 선반에 꽂혀 있는. · 고맙네.

Now let us consider the situation / and see / what may
이제 상황을 고려해 보고 · 알아보세

be deduced from it. In the first place, / we may start /
그로부터 뭘 추리할 수 있는지. · 우선, · 시작하지

with a strong presumption / that Colonel Openshaw had
강한 추측부터 · 오픈쇼 대령에게 중요한 이유가 있다는

some very strong reason / for leaving America. Men
미국을 떠나야 할.

at his time of life / do not change all their habits / and
남자는 사는 동안 · 습관을 바꾸지 않고

exchange willingly / the charming climate of Florida
교환하지 않을 거네 · 플로리다의 매력적인 기후를

/ for the lonely life of an English provincial town. His
영국 지방 도시의 외로운 생활과.

extreme love of solitude in England / suggests the idea
그가 영국에서 지나치게 고독했던 것은 · 의미하지

/ that he was in fear of someone or something, / so we
누군가 혹은 뭔가에 대한 공포를 느꼈다는 걸,

may assume / as a working hypothesis / that it was
그래서 추측할 수 있네 · 유력한 가설을

fear of someone or something / which drove him from
그 공포는 누군가 혹은 뭔가에 대한 것이라고 · 미국으로부터 온.

America. As to what it was he feared, / we can only
그가 두려워한 것이 뭐였냐에 대해서는, · 추론할 수 있을 뿐이지

deduce / that by considering the formidable letters /
그 무서운 편지에 대해 생각함으로써

which were received by himself and his successors. Did
그 자신과 후손에게 전해진.

you remark the postmarks of those letters?"
편지의 소인에 대해 말해 보겠나?"

"The first was from Pondicherry, / the second from
첫 번째는 퐁디셰리에서, 두 번째는 던디에서,

Dundee, / and the third from London."
그리고 세 번째는 런던에서 왔네."

"From East London. What do you deduce from that?"
"런던 동부이지. 거기에서 무엇을 추론하겠나?"

"They are all seaports. That the writer was on board of a
"모두 항구 도시로군. 쓴 사람은 배를 타고 있었네."

ship."

"Excellent. We have already a clue. There can be no
"훌륭해. 이미 단서 하나를 가졌네. 분명히

doubt / that the probability / — the strong probability —
가능성이 있지 — 높은 가능성이 —

/ is that the writer was on board of a ship. And now let
쓴 사람이 배에 타고 있을 거라는. 그럼 이제 생각해 보지

us consider / another point. In the case of Pondicherry,
다른 점을. 퐁디셰리의 경우엔,

/ seven weeks elapsed / between the threat and its
7주가 흘렀네 협박과 실제 사건 사이에,

fulfilment, / in Dundee / it was only some three or four
던디의 경우엔 사나흘 밖에 걸리지 않았지.

days. Does that suggest anything?"
이 사실이 암시하는 바가 있나?"

"A greater distance to travel."
"매우 먼 거리를 여행했다는 점."

"But the letter had also a greater distance to come."
"하지만 편지도 먼 거리에서 왔지."

"Then / I do not see the point."
"그럼 모르겠는데."

seaports 항구 도시 | vessel 선박 | steamer 증기선

64 The Five Orange Pips

"There is at least a presumption / that the vessel / in
"적어도 하나의 추론이 나오지   그 배는

which the man or men / are is a sailing-ship. It looks /
사람 혹은 사람들이 타고 있던   범선이라는 점이네.   보이지

as if they always send their singular warning or token
항상 특별한 경고나 신호를 보내는 것처럼

/ before them / when starting upon their mission. You
그 이전에   임무를 시작할 때.   알겠지

see / how quickly the deed followed the sign / when it
신호 뒤에 행동이 얼마나 빨리 일어났는지

came from Dundee. If they had come from Pondicherry
던디에서 협박이 왔을 때.   퐁디셰리에서 왔다면

/ in a steamer / they would have arrived / almost as soon
증기선을 타고   도착했겠지   거의 편지가 도착하자마자.

as their letter. But, / as a matter of fact, / seven weeks
하지만,   사실은,   7주가 걸렸네.

elapsed. I think / that those seven weeks represented the
내 생각에   7주라는 시간은 차이를 나타내지

difference / between the mail-boat / which brought the
우편선과   편지를 싣고 온

letter / and the sailing vessel / which brought the writer."
범선 사이의   글 쓴 사람을 데려오는."

"It is possible."
가능한 얘기군."

"More than that. It is probable. And now / you see / the
"그 이상이네.   아마 그럴 거네.   그럼 이제   알겠지

deadly urgency of this new case, / and why I urged /
이 사건의 긴급함을,   또 내가 왜 충고했는지

young Openshaw to caution. The blow has always fallen
오픈쇼에게 조심하라고.   공격은 항상 일어났네

/ at the end of the time / which it would take the senders
막바지에   발신자가 여행을 끝내는 데 걸리는 시간의.

to travel the distance. But this one comes from London, /
하지만 이건 런던에서 왔으니,

and therefore / we cannot count upon delay."
따라서   우리는 지체할 수 없네."

"Good God!" / I cried.
"하나님 맙소사!" 내가 소리쳤다.

"What can it mean, / this relentless persecution?"
"무슨 의미지, 이 무자비한 괴롭힘이?"

"The papers which Openshaw carried / are obviously
"오픈쇼가 가지고 있던 서류는

of vital importance / to the person or persons in the
분명히 중요한 것이네 배에 타고 있는 사람에게.

sailing-ship. I think that it is quite clear / that there
확실한 것 같네

must be more than one of them. A single man could
한 명 이상일 거라는 게. 한 사람이라면 실행할 수 없었을 테니

not have carried out / two deaths / in such a way / as to
두 건이 살인을 그런 방식으로

deceive a coroner's jury. There must have been several
검시 배심원을 속이는. 여러 명이 틀림없고,

in it, / and they must have been / men of resource and
그들은 틀림없이 지식과 결단력 있는 사람이네.

determination. Their papers / they mean to have, / be
그 서류를 그들은 손에 넣으려 하는 거야,

the holder of them who it may. In this way / you see /
가지고 있는 자가 누구든. 이런 식으로 자네도 알 수 있지

K. K. K. ceases to be the initials of an individual / and
K. K. K.가 개인의 이름 이니셜이 아니라

becomes the badge of a society."
단체의 상징이 된다는 것을."

"But of what society?"
"하지만 어떤 단체 말인가?"

"Have you never —" / said Sherlock Holmes, / bending
"자네는 —" 홈즈가 말했다,

forward / and sinking his voice — / "have you never
몸을 숙이고 목소리를 낮추며 — "자네는 들어본 적 있나

heard / of the Ku Klux Klan?"
쿠 클럭스 클랜에 대해? "

---

relentless 무자비한 | persecution 학대, 괴롭힘 | coroner's jury 검시 배심(사인을 평결함)

"I never have."
"없네."

Holmes turned over the leaves of the book / upon his
홈즈는 책장을 넘겼다   무릎 위에 있던.

knee.

"Here it is," / said he presently:
"여기 있네,"   곧 말했다:

"'Ku Klux Klan. A name derived / from the fanciful
" '쿠 클럭스 클랜.   유래한 이름이다   닮았다는 점에서 착안한

resemblance / to the sound produced by cocking a rifle.
소총을 당길 때 나는 소리와.

This terrible secret society was formed / by some ex-
이 무서운 비밀 집단은 만들어졌다

*Confederate soldiers / in the Southern states / after
전직 남부연합 군인들에 의해   남부에서

the Civil War, / and it rapidly formed local branches / in
남북전쟁 이후,   그리고 빠르게 거점을 넓혀갔다

different parts of the country, / notably / in Tennessee,
미국 다른 도시로,   특히

Louisiana, the Carolinas, Georgia, and Florida. Its power
테네시, 루이지애나, 캐롤라이나, 조지아, 그리고 플로리다 등에서.

was used for political purposes, / principally for the
그들의 힘은 정치적 목적을 위해 사용되었는데,   주로 흑인 유권자들을 습격하거나

terrorising of the negro voters / and the murdering / and
죽이거나

driving from the country / of those who were opposed
지역으로부터 추방했다   이들의 생각에 반대하는 사람들을.

to its views. Its outrages were usually preceded / by a
폭력에 앞서

warning sent / to the marked man / in some fantastic but
경고를 보냈다   표적이 된 사람에게

---

fanciful 상상의 | notably 특히 | terrorise 공포에 떨게 하다(=terrorize) | precede ~에 앞서다 | sprig 잔가지 |
abjure 포기하다 | with impunity 벌을 받지 않고, 무사히 | perpetrator 가해자 | sporadic 산발적인

generally recognised shape / — a sprig of oak-leaves in
기이하지만 알아볼 수 있는 형태로 — 어떤 지역에서는 떡갈나무의 가지를,

some parts, / melon seeds or orange pips in others. On
다른 지역에서는 멜론이나 오렌지 씨앗을 사용하여.

receiving this / the victim might either openly abjure /
이를 받으면 희생자는 공개적으로 포기하거나

his former ways, / or might fly from the country. If he
자신의 방식을, 혹은 그 지역에서 도망쳤다.

braved the matter out, / death would unfailingly come
만약 용감하게 그 문제를 공개하면, 반드시 죽음이 그를 찾아갔다,

upon him, / and usually in some strange and unforeseen
대개 이상하고 예측할 수 없는 방식으로.

manner. So perfect was the organisation of the society,
모임의 조직이 매우 완벽했고,

/ and so systematic its methods, / that there is hardly a
방법이 매우 체계적이어서, 거의 기록된 사건이 없다

case upon record / where any man succeeded / in braving
누군가가 성공한 사례에 대한

it with impunity, / or in which any of its outrages / were
대항하여 무사했거나, 혹은 이들의 폭력 행동에 대해

traced home to the perpetrators. For some years / the
가해자를 추적했다는. 몇 년 동안

organisation flourished / in spite of the efforts / of the
조직은 번성했다 노력에도 불구하고

United States government / and of the better classes
미국 정부와 남부 상류층이 기울였던.

of the community in the South. Eventually, / in the
결국,

year 1869, / the movement rather suddenly collapsed, /
1869년에, 이 운동은 갑자기 붕괴했다,

although there have been sporadic outbreaks of the same
하지만 비슷한 종류의 사건이 산발적으로 발생했다

sort / since that date.'"
그 이후에.' "

---

* 아메리카 남부연합(Confederate States of America)을 뜻함. 미국 남북전쟁 때 합중국을 탈퇴한
남부 11주가 결성한 국가(1861~1865)로 수도는 리치먼드이다.

"You will observe," / said Holmes, / laying down the
"자네도 알겠지만," 홈즈가 말했다, 책을 내려 놓으며,

volume, / "that the sudden breaking up of the society /
"갑작스런 조직의 붕괴는

was coincident / with the disappearance of Openshaw
일치하네 오픈쇼가 미국으로부터 사라진 때와

from America / with their papers. It may well have been
서류를 갖고. 있는 게 분명해

/ cause and effect. It is no wonder / that he and his family
인과 관계가. 놀랄 일도 아니지 오픈쇼와 가족이 당하게 된 것도

have / some of the more implacable spirits upon their
그들의 더욱 완강한 추적을.

track. You can understand / that this register and diary
이해하겠지 명부와 일기에 나타나 있는 거야

may implicate / some of the first men in the South, / and
남부 최고위층의 이름이,

that there may be many / who will not sleep easy at night
그러니 많이 있을 거네 밤에 편히 잠자지 못하는 사람들이

/ until it is recovered."
이 서류를 되찾을 때까지."

"Then the page we have seen —"
"그럼 우리가 본 종이가 —"

"Is such as we might expect. It ran, / if I remember right,
"우리가 추리한 대로 일 거야.   거기에는,   내 기억이 맞는다면,

/ 'sent the pips to A, B, and C' / — that is, / sent the
'A, B, C에게 씨앗 발송' 이라 쓰여 있었네   — 즉,

society's warning to them. Then / there are successive
경고를 보냈다는 거지.   그리고 나서 성공한 목록이 나오지

entries / that A and B cleared, / or left the country, /
          A와 B 제거,   혹은 미국을 떠남

and finally that C was visited, with, / I fear, / a sinister
그리고 C를 방문했다고,   내 생각엔,   C에게는 끔찍한

result for C. Well, I think, / Doctor, / that we may let
결과가 있었겠지.   내 생각에,   의사 양반,   빛을 약간 준 것 같은데

some light / into this dark place, / and I believe / that
          이 어두운 장소에,   그리고 내가 알기에

the only chance young Openshaw has / in the meantime
오픈쇼에게 유일한 기회는   그 동안

/ is to do / what I have told him. There is nothing more
          하는 것이네   내가 말한 대로.   더 이상 없네

/ to be said or to be done / to-night, / so hand me over
          할 말도 할 일도   오늘 밤,   그러니 내 바이올린을 건네 주고

my violin / and let us try to forget / for half an hour / the
잊어보세   30분 만이라도

miserable weather / and the still more miserable ways of
이 우울한 날씨와   우리 의뢰인의 더욱 비참한 행보에 대해서도."

our fellow-men."

coincident 일치하는 | implacable 확고한, 바꿀 수 없는 | implicate (범죄에) 연루되었음을 보여 주다 |
fellow-men 동포

A. 다음 문장을 해석해 보세요.

(1) Carefully as I examined / every fact connected with his death, / I was unable to find anything / which could suggest the idea of murder.

→

(2) I was well convinced / that our troubles were / in some way / dependent upon an incident in my uncle's life, / and that the danger would be as pressing / in one house / as in another.

→

(3) This strange, wild story seemed to have come to us / from amid the mad elements / — blown in upon us / like a sheet of sea-weed in a gale — / and now to have been reabsorbed / by them / once more.

→

(4) So perfect was the organisation of the society, / and so systematic its methods, / that there is hardly a case upon record / where any man succeeded in braving it / with impunity, / or in which any of its outrages / were traced home to the perpetrators.

→

B. 다음 주어진 문구가 알맞은 문장이 되도록 순서를 맞춰 보세요.

(1) 내가 해시계나 서류랑 무슨 상관이 있지?
   (with / to do / What / I / sundials and papers / have)
   →

(2) 그런 말도 안 되는 일엔 신경 쓰지 않을 테다.
   (I / no / such / take / of / shall / notice / nonsense)
   →

A. (1) 아버지의 죽음과 관련된 모든 사항을 자세히 조사했지만, 타살을 암시하는 듯한 단서를 아무것도 알아 낼 수 없었다. (2) 우리 집 문제는 어떤 면에서 큰아버지의 삶 속의 어떤 사건과 관계가 있기 때문에 위험은 우리 집에서나 다른 집에 가서나 마찬가지일 거라고 확신하고 있다. (3) 이 기이하고 터무니없는 이야기는 사나운 자연으로부터 강풍에 실린 해초처럼 우리에게 날아 들어 찾아왔다가 이제 다시 한 번 자연으로 빨려 들

(3) 힘을 내야만 살아날 수 있소.
(can / save / Nothing / you / energy / but)
→

(4) 할 일은 한 가지밖에 없소.
(do / but / thing / to / is / There / one)
→

C. 다음 주어진 문장이 본문의 내용과 맞으면 T, 틀리면 F에 동그라미 하세요.

(1) John Openshaw made a careful examination of the attic, but he couldn't find anything.
(T / F)

(2) The father of John Openshaw passed away by falling over the bridge.
(T / F)

(3) John Openshaw didn't go to the police because he thought they didn't believe him.
(T / F)

(4) Sherlock Holmes decided to start work upon Openshaw's case in London.
(T / F)

D. 의미가 비슷한 것끼리 서로 연결해 보세요.

(1) preposterous   ▶   ◀ ① ask

(2) imminent   ▶   ◀ ② unreasonable

(3) implore   ▶   ◀ ③ tremendous

(4) formidable   ▶   ◀ ④ near

어간 것 같았다. (4) 그 모임의 조직이 매우 완벽하고 방법이 매우 체계적이어서, 누군가 이들에게 대항하여 무사히 성공했거나, 이들의 폭력 행동에 대해 가해자를 추적했다는 기록이 거의 없다. | B. (1) What have I to do with sundials and papers? (2) I shall take no notice of such nonsense. (3) Nothing but energy can save you. (4) There is but one thing to do. | C. (1) F (2) F (3) F (4) T | D. (1) ② (2) ④ (3) ① (4) ③

73

3

It had cleared / in the morning, / and the sun was shining
날이 개었고　　　　아침에,　　　　태양이 빛나고 있었다

/ with a subdued brightness / through the dim veil /
빛을 뿌리며　　　　　　　　희미한 장막 같은 구름을 뚫고

which hangs over the great city. Sherlock Holmes was
대도시 위에 드리워진.　　　　　　셜록 홈즈는 이미 아침 식사 중이었다

already at breakfast / when I came down.
　　　　　　　　　　내가 내려왔을 때.

"You will excuse me / for not waiting for you," / said
"용서하게　　　　　자네를 기다리지 않아서,"　　　그가 말했다;

he; / "I have, / I foresee, / a very busy day before me / in
　"내게,　　예상하기에,　　매우 바쁜 하루가 될 것 같아서

looking into this case of young Openshaw's."
오픈쇼 사건을 조사하느라고."

"What steps will you take?" / I asked.
"어떤 조치를 취할 건가?"　　　　내가 물었다.

"It will very much depend / upon the results of my first
"달려 있지　　　　　　　　첫 번째 조사 결과에.

inquiries. I may have to go down to Horsham, / after all."
　　　　　호섬에 가야 할지도 모르지,　　　　　결국."

"You will not go there first?"
"호섬에 먼저 가는 게 아니고?"

"No, / I shall commence with the City. Just ring the bell /
"아니,　여기에서 시작할 거네.　　　　　　　초인종을 울리게

and the maid will bring up your coffee."
그러면 하녀가 커피를 가져올 거야."

As I waited, / I lifted the unopened newspaper / from
기다리면서,　　나는 접혀 있던 신문을 들어

the table / and glanced my eye over it. It rested upon a
탁자에서　　　훑어보았다.　　　　　　어떤 기사 제목에 시선이

heading / which sent a chill to my heart.
머물렀다　　가슴 철렁하게 만든.

---

subdued 가라앉은, 좀 우울한 | take steps 조치를 취하다 | commence 시작하다 | rest upon[on] ~에 시선이
머물다

"Holmes," / I cried, / "you are too late."
"홈즈," 내가 소리쳤다, "자네가 너무 늦었군."

"Ah!" / said he, / laying down his cup, / "I feared as
"아!" 그가 말했다, 컵을 내려놓으며, "그럴 까봐 염려했지.

much. How was it done?"
어떻게 된 건가?"

He spoke calmly, / but I could see / that he was deeply
그는 조용히 말했지만, 볼 수 있었다 심히 동요하는 모습을.

moved.

"My eye caught the name of Openshaw, / and the
"오픈쇼라는 이름이 시선을 사로잡았어,

heading 'Tragedy Near Waterloo Bridge.' Here is the
'워털루 다리의 비극' 이라는 제목과.

account:
내용을 읽어 주지:

Between nine and ten / last night / Police-Constable
9시에서 10시 사이에 어젯밤 컨스터블 쿡 경관은,

Cook, / of the H Division, / on duty near Waterloo
H지구대 소속, 워털루 다리 근처에서 근무 중이던,

Bridge, / heard a cry for help / and a splash in the water.
도와달라는 외침을 들었다 물이 튀는 소리와.

The night, / however, / was extremely dark and stormy,
그날 밤은, 하지만, 무척 어둡고 폭풍이 거세었고,

/ so that, / in spite of the help of several passers-by, /
그래서, 지나가던 행인들의 도움에도 불구하고,

it was quite impossible to effect a rescue. The alarm, /
구조는 불가능했다. 경보가,

however, / was given, / and, / by the aid of the water-
그러나, 울리고, 그리고, 수상 경찰의 도움으로,

police, / the body was eventually recovered. It proved
마침내 시신을 수습할 수 있었다. 밝혀졌다

/ to be that of a young gentleman / whose name, / as
시신은 젊은 신사였고 이름은,

it appears from an envelope / which was found in his
봉투에 나타난 대로   주머니에서 발견된,

pocket, / was John Openshaw, / and whose residence is
존 오픈쇼인 것으로,   호셤 근처 주민인.

near Horsham. It is conjectured / that he may have been
추정된다   그는 서둘러 가는 중이었고

hurrying down / to catch the last train / from Waterloo
막차를 잡기 위해   워털루 역에서 출발하는,

Station, / and that in his haste / and the extreme darkness
서두른 데다가   너무 어두워서

/ he missed his path / and walked over / the edge of one
발을 헛디디고   추락한 듯 하다   작은 선착장 끝에서

of the small landing-places / for river steamboats. The
증기선용의.

body exhibited no traces of violence, / and there can be
시체에는 폭행의 흔적이 없었기에,

no doubt / that the deceased had been the victim / of an
의심할 바 없이   고인은 희생된 것이 분명하다

unfortunate accident, / which should have the effect / of
불운한 사고로,   이 사고로 인하여

calling the attention of the authorities / to the condition
당국이 주의가 요구된다

of the riverside landing-stages."
강변 선착장의 상태를 점검하도록."

We sat in silence / for some minutes, / Holmes more
우리는 말 없이 앉아 있었다   몇 분 동안,   홈즈는 가장 침울하고

depressed and shaken / than I had ever seen him.
동요하는 모습이었다   지금까지 보아왔던 것 중.

"That hurts my pride, / Watson," / he said at last.
"내 자존심에 상처를 입혔군,   왓슨,"   마침내 그가 말했다.

fear ~일까 염려하다 | deceased 사망한

"It is a petty feeling, / no doubt, / but it hurts my pride.
"편협한 감정이겠지만, 물론, 자존심이 상처를 입었어.

It becomes a personal matter / with me / now, / and, /
이 사건은 개인의 문제가 되었네 내게 이제, 그리고,

if God sends me health, / I shall set my hand upon this
신이 건강을 허락하는 한, 내 손으로 이 패거리를 잡고 말 거네.

gang. That he should come to me for help, / and that I
그는 내게 도움을 청하러 왔는데,

should send him away to his death — !"
내가 그를 죽음으로 내몰다니 — !"

He sprang from his chair / and paced about the room / in
그는 의자에서 벌떡 일어나 방 안을 걸어다녔다

uncontrollable agitation, / with a flush upon his sallow
주체할 수 없이 동요하며, 두 뺨이 붉게 달아오른 채

cheeks / and a nervous clasping and unclasping of his
길고 가는 손을 불안한 듯 쥐었다 폈다 하면서.

long thin hands.

---

* 웨스트민스터 다리에서 블랙프라이스 다리까지 약 2km에 걸친 템즈강 북쪽 둑길 '빅토리아 임뱅
크먼트'를 뜻한다.

"They must be cunning devils," / he exclaimed at last.
"교활한 악당이 틀림없어,"   그가 마침내 외쳤다.

"How could they have decoyed him / down there? The
"어떻게 그를 유인한 거지   그 아래로?

*Embankment is not on the direct line to the station.
그 둑길은 역으로 가는 지름길이 아니야.

The bridge, / no doubt, / was too crowded, / even on such
다리는,   틀림없이,   붐볐을 거고,   그런 밤이라도,

a night, / for their purpose. Well, Watson, / we shall see
그 용도로 볼 때.   음, 왓슨,   누가 이기는지

who will win / in the long run. I am going out now!"
두고보자고   결국.   이제 나가야겠네!"

"To the police?"
"경찰서로?"

"No; / I shall be my own police. When I have spun the
"아니;   내가 경찰이 되겠네.   내가 거미줄을 쳐 놓으면

web / they may take the flies, / but not before."
경찰들은 파리를 잡을 수 있겠지만,   그 전엔 안 될 걸."

All day / I was engaged in my professional work, / and
하루 종일   나는 환자를 돌보았고,

it was late in the evening / before I returned to Baker
늦은 밤이 되어서야   베이커 가로 돌아갔다.

Street. Sherlock Holmes had not come back yet. It was
홈즈는 아직 돌아오지 않은 채였다.

nearly ten o'clock / before he entered, / looking pale
10시가 다 되어서야   그가 돌아왔다,   창백하고 지친 모습으로,

and worn. He walked up to the sideboard, / and tearing
그는 찬장으로 걸어가서,

a piece from the loaf / he devoured it voraciously, /
빵 한 조각을 떼어,   게걸스럽게 먹더니,

washing it down with a long draught of water.
물 한 잔을 들이켜 빵을 넘겼다.

---

agitation 불안, 동요 | sallow 약간 누런, 병색이 엿보이는 | clasping 움켜쥐기 | decoy 유인하다 | spin (실을)
잣다 | voraciously 게걸스럽게

"You are hungry," / I remarked.
"배가 고팠군," 내가 말했다.

"Starving. It had escaped my memory. I have had
"굶어 죽을 뻔 했지. 먹어야겠다는 생각이 안 들더군.

nothing since breakfast."
아침 이후로 아무것도 못 먹었네."

"Nothing?"
"아무것도?"

"Not a bite. I had no time to think of it."
"한 조각도. 먹을 것을 생각할 시간이 없었어."

"And how have you succeeded?"
"그럼 어떻게 되었나?"

"Well."
"잘 됐지."

"You have a clue?"
"단서는 찾았나?"

"I have them in the hollow of my hand. Young
"그들은 이제 내 손바닥 위에 있네.

Openshaw shall not long remain unavenged. Why, /
머지않아 오픈쇼의 복수를 하게 될 거네. 자,

Watson, / let us put their own devilish trade-mark / upon
왓슨, 그들의 악마 같은 징표를 보내도록 하지

them. It is well thought of!"
그들에게. 정말 좋은 생각이지!"

"What do you mean?"
"무슨 말인가?"

---

* 미국 조지아 주 남동부 서배너 강 하구에 있는 항구도시. 조지아주 최고의 관광중심지이고, 공업
도시이자 미국 남동부의 주요 무역항이다.

thrust 밀다, 찌르다 | precursor 선구자

He took an orange / from the cupboard, / and tearing it
그는 오렌지 하나를 꺼내   찬장에서,   조각조각 찢어서

to pieces / he squeezed out the pips / upon the table. Of
씨를 발라내더니   탁자 위에 놓았다.

these / he took five / and thrust them into an envelope.
이 중에서 다섯 개를 집더니   봉투 안에 찔러 넣었다.

On the inside of the flap / he wrote "S. H. for J. O."
봉투 안쪽에   'J. O.를 대신해서 S. H.가' 라고 썼다.

Then he sealed it / and addressed it / to "Captain James
그리고 나서 봉투를 붙인 후   주소를 썼다   '제임스 칼훈 선장 앞,

Calhoun, / Barque Lone Star, / *Savannah, Georgia."
범선 론스타 호,   조지아 주 서배너함' 이라고.

"That will await him / when he enters port," / said he, /
"이 편지가 그를 기다리겠지   그가 항구에 도착하면,"   홈즈가 말했다,

chuckling.
웃으며.

"It may give him / a sleepless night. He will find it / as
"이 편지가 선사하겠지   잠들지 못하는 밤을.   알게 될 거야

sure a precursor of his fate / as Openshaw did before
자신의 운명에 대한 전조라고   오픈쇼에게 닥친 것처럼."

him."

"And who is this Captain Calhoun?"
"그런데 이 칼훈 선장은 누군가?"

"The leader of the gang. I shall have the others, / but he
"그 악당의 우두머리이지.   다른 놈들도 처리하겠지만,   이 자가

first."
먼저야."

"How did you trace it, / then?"
"어떻게 추적한 거야,   그럼?"

He took a large sheet of paper / from his pocket, / all
홈즈는 커다란 종이 한 장을 꺼냈다   주머니에서,

covered with dates and names.
날짜와 이름이 가득 적혀 있는.

"I have spent the whole day," / said he, / "over Lloyd's
"하루 종일 보냈지," 그가 말했다. "로이드 선박 등록부와

registers and files of the old papers, / following the future
오래된 서류철을 뒤지며,

career of every vessel / which touched at Pondicherry /
모든 선박들의 예정 항로를 쫓아서 퐁디셰리 항에 정박했던

in January and February in '83. There were thirty-six
1883년 1월과 2월에. 법정 용적을 지킨 배는 36척이 있었네

ships of fair tonnage / which were reported there / during
거기에 보고된

those months. Of these, / one, / the Lone Star, / instantly
그 기간 동안. 이 중에서, 한 척, 론스타 호가,

attracted my attention, / since, / although it was reported
곧 내 주의를 끌었지, 왜냐하면, 기록되어 있지만

/ as having cleared from London, / the name is that /
런던에서 출발했다고, 배 이름은

which is given to one of the states of the Union."
미국의 어느 주의 이름이니까."

"Texas, / I think."
"텍사스지, 내 생각엔."

"I was not / and am not sure / which; / but I knew / that
"난 몰랐고 지금도 확실히 모르네 어느 주인지; 하지만 알았네

the ship must have an American origin."
그 배가 미국에서 온 선박이 분명하다는 사실을."

"What then?"
"그 다음엔?"

"I searched the Dundee records, / and when I found / that
"던디 항의 기록을 찾았지, 그리고 찾아냈을 때

the barque Lone Star was there / in January, '85, / my
범선 론스타 호가 그곳에 있었다는 기록을 1885년 1월에,

suspicion became a certainty. I then / inquired as to the
내 의심이 확실해졌지. 그 다음에 배에 대해 조사했네

vessels / which lay at present / in the port of London."
지금 정박해 있는 런던 항에."

---

tonnage (선박의) 용적 톤수 | barque 바크형 범선(돛대가 세 개 이상인 범선)

"Yes?"
"그래?"

"The Lone Star had arrived here / last week. I went
"론스타 호는 이곳에 도착했네   지난주에.

down to the Albert Dock / and found / that she had been
앨버트 부두에 가서   알게 됐지   그 배는 이미 강을 내려가서

taken down the river / by the early tide this morning, /
오늘 아침 썰물을 타고,

homeward bound to Savannah. I wired to **Gravesend** /
서배너 항으로.   나는 그레이브센드에 전보를 쳐서

and learned / that she had passed / some time ago, / and
알았네   배가 통과했다는 것을   몇 시간 전에,

as the wind is easterly / I have no doubt / that she is now
그리고 동풍이 불고 있으니까   틀림없이

past the Goodwins / and not very far from the Isle of
지금 굿윈스를 지나서   와이트 섬에서 멀지 않은 곳에 있을 거야."

Wight."

"What will you do, / then?"
"어떻게 할 건가,   그럼?"

"Oh, I have my hand upon him. He and the two mates,
"오, 그에게 손을 써 뒀지.   그 놈과 동료 두 명은,

/ are as I learn, / the only native-born Americans / in
알아보니,   유일한 미국 출신이네

the ship. The others are Finns and Germans. I know, /
그 배에서.   다른 사람들은 핀란드와 독일 출신이지.   알아냈네,

also, / that they were all three away from the ship / last
또한,   그 세 명 모두 배에 없었다는 사실을

night. I had it from the stevedore / who has been loading
어젯밤에. 이 정보는 부두 일꾼에게 얻었지   그 배의 짐을 싣고 있던.

their cargo. By the time that their sailing-ship reaches
그 배가 서배너 항에 도착할 때까지

Savannah / the mail-boat will have carried this letter, /
우편선이 이 편지를 싣고 갈 것이고,

and the cable will have informed the police of Savannah
전보로 서배너 항에 대해 경찰에 알릴 거네

/ that these three gentlemen are badly wanted here / upon
이 세 남자가 이곳에서 수배되었다고

a charge of murder."
살인죄로."

There is ever a flaw, / however, / in the best laid of
결함이 있는 법이다   하지만   인간이 세운 계획에는,

human plans, / and the murderers of John Openshaw
그래서 존 오픈쇼를 죽인 살인자들은

were / never to receive the orange pips / which would
결국 오렌지 씨앗을 받지 못했다   그들에게 알려 줄

show them / that another, / as cunning and as resolute as
다른 자가,   그들 자신만큼이나 교활하고 단호한,

themselves, / was upon their track. Very long and very
뒤쫓고 있다는 사실을.   매우 오랫동안 거세게

severe / were the equinoctial gales / that year. We waited
폭풍이 몰아쳤다   그 해에는.   우리는 오래 기다

long / for news of the Lone Star of Savannah, / but none
렸지만,   서배너 항에 론스타 호가 도착했다는 소식을

ever reached us. We did at last hear / that somewhere far
아무 소식도 없었다.   우리는 마침내 듣게 됐다   먼 대서양 어느 곳에서

out in the Atlantic / a shattered stern-post of a boat / was
부서진 배 꼬리의 파편이

seen swinging in the trough of a wave, / with the letters
파도 사이를 떠다닌다는 소식을,

"L. S." carved upon it, / and that is / all which we shall
'L. S' 라는 글자가 새겨진   그리고 이것이   우리가 알게 된 전부이다

ever know / of the fate of the Lone Star.
론스타 호의 운명에 대해.

* 그레이브센드 : 런던 항의 관문으로 알려진 템즈 강변의 항구 도시

stevedore 부두 일꾼, 항만 노동자 | cable 전보를 보내다 | flaw 결함 | resolute 단호한 | stern-post 선미재(船尾材), 배의 꼬리 부분 구조물 | trough (파도, 산등성이 사이의) 골

A. 다음 문장을 해석해 보세요.

(1) It proved to be that of a young gentleman / whose name, / as it appears from an envelope / which was found in his pocket, / was John Openshaw, / and whose residence is near Horsham.
→

(2) The body exhibited no traces of violence, / and there can be no doubt / that the deceased had been the victim / of an unfortunate accident.
→

(3) The bridge, / no doubt, / was too crowded, / even on such a night, / for their purpose.
→

(4) There is ever a flaw, / however, / in the best laid of human plans, / and the murderers of John Openshaw were / never to receive the orange pips / which would show them / that another, / as cunning and as resolute as themselves, / was upon their track.
→

B. 다음 주어진 문장이 되도록 빈칸에 써 넣으세요.

(1) 그럴 까봐 염려했지.

→

(2) 신이 내게 건강을 허락하는 한 내 손으로 이 패거리를 잡고 말 거네.

→

(3) 그들은 이제 내 손바닥 위에 있네.

→

A. (1) 그의 주머니에서 발견된 봉투에 적힌 대로, 호섬 근처의 주민인 존 오픈쇼라는 이름의 젊은 신사의 시신으로 밝혀졌다. (2) 시체에는 폭행의 흔적이 없었기에, 의심할 바 없이 고인은 불운한 사고로 희생된 것이 분명하다. (3) 그 다리는 그 용도로 볼 때 그런 밤이라도 틀림없이 붐볐을 것이다. (4) 하지만 인간이 세운 계획에는 결함이 있는 법이고, 그래서 존 오픈쇼를 죽인 살인자들은 그들 자신 만큼이나 교활하고 단호한 다

(4) 그들의 악마 같은 징표를 그들에게 보내도록 하지.

→

C. 다음 주어진 문구가 알맞은 문장이 되도록 순서를 맞춰 보세요.

(1) 구조는 불가능했다.
(effect / It was / to / a rescue / impossible / quite)
→

(2) 그는 내게 도움을 청하러 왔는데, <u>내가 그를 죽음으로 내몰다니!</u>
(I / to / death / him / away / send / his / should)
That he should come to me for help, and that ⬚⬚⬚⬚⬚⬚
⬚⬚⬚⬚⬚⬚⬚⬚⬚⬚⬚⬚⬚.

(3) 그 생각이 전혀 안 나더군.
(escaped / It / my memory / had)
→

(4) 머지 않아 오픈쇼 청년의 복수를 하게 될 거네.
(long / Young Openshaw / unavenged / shall / remain / not)
→

D. 다음 단어에 대한 맞는 설명과 연결해 보세요.

(1) agitation ▶ ◀ ① intended to attract people's attentionvery

(2) decoy ▶ ◀ ② push or move quickly

(3) thrust ▶ ◀ ③ undesirable quality

(4) flaw ▶ ◀ ④ worried state

The Adventure of the Blue Carbuncle

푸른 카벙클

I had called upon my friend Sherlock Holmes / upon the
나는 친구 셜록 홈즈의 집에 들렀다

second morning after Christmas, / with the intention
크리스마스 다음 다음 날 아침에,   새해 인사나 전할 생각으로,

of wishing him the compliments of the season. He was

lounging upon the sofa / in a purple dressing-gown, / a
그는 소파에 느긋하게 앉아 있었다   자주색 실내복을 입은 채,

pipe-rack within his reach / upon the right, / and a pile
파이프 걸이는 손 닿는 곳에 놓여 있고   오른쪽에,

of crumpled morning papers, / evidently newly studied,
구겨진 조간신문은 쌓여 있었다,   최근 살펴본 게 분명한,

/ near at hand. Beside the couch / was a wooden chair,
   주위에.   소파 옆에는   나무 의자가 하나 있었는데,

/ and on the angle of the back / hung a very seedy and
   의자 등받이에   지저분하고 형편없는 펠트 모자가 걸려

disreputable hard-felt hat, / much the worse for wear,
있었다,   쓰고 다니기에 너무 낡았고,

/ and cracked in several places. A lens and a forceps /
   군데군데 갈라진.   확대경과 겸자로

lying upon the seat of the chair / suggested / that the hat
의자 위에 놓여 있는   짐작할 수 있었다

had been suspended / in this manner / for the purpose of
그 모자가 걸려 있는 것이   이런 방식으로   조사하기 위한 것임을.

examination.

---

* 카벙클 : 모난 곳이 없이 둥글게 다듬은 석류석을 말하며, 보통 가넷(garnet)이라 부른다. 석류석
은 흰색, 노락색, 초록색, 빨간색 등 여러 가지 색이 있지만, 푸른색의 석류석은 보고된 바가 없다.

call upon 방문하다, 들르다 | lounge 느긋하게 서 있다, 앉아 있다 | crumpled 뒤틀린, 쭈글쭈글한,
주름살투성이의 | newly 최근데, 새로 | seedy 지저분한, 더러운 | disreputable 평판이 안 좋은, 형편 없는 |
forcep 겸자(의사들이 쓰는 날이 없는 기다란 가위같이 생긴 도구) | interrupt 방해하다 | jerk 확 움직이다, 갑자기
쳐다보다 | devoid of ~이 없는 | crackling 탁탁하는 소리 | homely 매력 없는, 못생긴

"You are engaged," / said I; / "perhaps I interrupt you."
"일하는 중이군." 내가 말했다; "내가 방해했는지 모르겠네."

"Not at all. I am glad to have a friend / with whom I can
"전혀. 친구가 와서 기쁘다네 조사 결과에 대해 이야기

discuss my results. The matter is a perfectly trivial one" /
나눌 수 있는. 문제는 매우 사소한 것이지만"

— he jerked his thumb / in the direction of the old hat —
— 그는 엄지손가락을 들어 낡은 모자를 가리켰다 —

/ "but there are points in connection with it / which are
"하지만 관계된 점이 있네

not entirely devoid / of interest and even of instruction."
전혀 없다고는 할 수 없는 흥미롭거나 심지어 교훈적이기까지 한."

I seated myself in his armchair / and warmed my hands
나는 안락의자에 앉아서 손을 쬐었다

/ before his crackling fire, / for a sharp frost had set in, /
탁탁 소리를 내는 난로에, 매서운 한파가 몰아쳐서,

and the windows were thick with the ice crystals.
창문에는 두꺼운 성에가 끼어 있었다.

"I suppose," / I remarked, / "that, homely as it looks, /
"내 생각엔," 내가 말했다, "볼품없어 보이지만,

this thing has some deadly story / linked on to it / — that
이 모자는 뭔가 무서운 사연을 가지고 있는 듯하군 모자에 관련된 — 단서인

it is the clue / which will guide you / in the solution of
거지 자네를 인도하게 될 수수께끼를 해결하고

some mystery / and the punishment of some crime."
범죄자를 처벌하도록."

"No, no. No crime," / said Sherlock Holmes, / laughing.
"아니, 아니야. 범죄는 아니네," 셜록 홈즈가 말했다, 웃으며.

"Only one of those whimsical little incidents / which will
엉뚱하고 사소한 사건 중 하나일 뿐이지   일어날 수 있는

happen / when you have four million human beings all
           4백만 명의 인간들이 겨루는 동안

jostling / each other / within the space of a few square
서로   몇 평방 마일의 공간 안에서.

miles. Amid the action and reaction / of so dense a
행동과 반사행동 가운데   그토록 빽빽하게 모여 있는

swarm of humanity, / every possible combination of
인간들의,   수많은 사건들의 조합이

events / may be expected to take place, / and many a
일어날 수 있으니까.   수많은 사소한 문제들도

little problem / will be presented / which may be striking
          나타날 수 있고   놀랍고 기괴한

and bizarre / without being criminal. We have already
범죄가 아니더라도.

had experience of such."
우린 이미 그런 경험을 해 봤지."

"So much so," / I remarked, / "that of the last six cases
"그건 그래,"   내가 말했다,   "지난 여섯 건의 사건 중에도

/ which I have added to my notes, / three have been
내가 기록한,

entirely free of any legal crime."
세 건은 법적으로 전혀 범죄가 아니었으니까."

"Precisely. You allude to / my attempt to recover the
"그렇네.   자네는 말하는 것이군   아이린 애들러의 사진을 되찾으려던 사건과,

Irene Adler papers, / to the singular case of Miss Mary
          메리 서덜랜드 양의 특이한 사건,

Sutherland, / and to the adventure of the man / with
          그리고 남자의 모험에 대해

the twisted lip. Well, / I have no doubt / that this small
삐뚤어진 입술을 가진.   그런데,   틀림없이   이 사소한 사건도

matter / will fall into the same innocent category. You
          같은 유형이 될 거네.

know Peterson, / the commissionaire?"
자네 피터슨을 알고 있지,   수위인?"

whimsical 엉뚱한, 기발한 | jostling 겨루는, 미는 | dense 빽빽한, 밀집한 | swarm 떼, 군중 | free of ~이 없는 | allude 암시하다, 언급하다 | commissionaire 수위

93

"Yes."
"알지."

"It is to him / that this trophy belongs."
"그의 것이라네   이 전리품은."

"It is his hat."
"그의 모자인가 보군."

"No, no, / he found it. Its owner is unknown. I beg that
"아니,   그가 발견한 것이지. 주인은 알 수 없어.

you will look upon it / not as a battered billycock / but
자네가 그걸 여겨 주길 바라네   낡은 중절모가 아니라

as an intellectual problem. And, / first, / as to how it
하나의 지적인 문제로써.   그럼,   먼저,   어떻게 여기까지 왔는지에

came here. It arrived upon Christmas morning, / in
대해 이야기하지.   모자는 크리스마스 날 아침에 도착했네,

company with a good fat goose, / which is, / I have no
살진 거위 한 마리와 함께,   그 거위는,   틀림없이,

doubt, / roasting at this moment / in front of Peterson's
지금 구워지고 있을 거야   피터슨의 화덕에서.

fire. The facts are these: / about four o'clock / on
사건의 진상은 이렇다네: 4시 쯤

Christmas morning, / Peterson, / who, / as you know,
크리스마스 날 아침,   피터슨이,   그는,   자네도 알다시피,

/ is a very honest fellow, / was returning from some
매우 정직한 사람인데,   한 잔 한 후 돌아가려고

small jollification / and was making his way homeward
                    집을 향해 걷고 있었다네

/ down Tottenham Court Road. In front of him / he saw,
토튼햄 코트 로드를 따라.   그의 앞에   보였지,

/ in the gaslight, / a tallish man, / walking with a slight
가스등 불빛 아래,   키 큰 사나이가,   약간 비틀거리며 걷는 모습이,

stagger, / and carrying a white goose / slung over his
            하얀 거위 한 마리를 메고   어깨 위에.

shoulder. As he reached the corner of Goodge Street, /
그가 구지 가 모퉁이에 이르렀을 때,

94   The Adventure of the Blue Carbuncle

a row broke out / between this stranger and a little knot
소란이 벌어졌네   이 낯선 이와 불량배 청년들 사이에.

of roughs. One of the latter / knocked off the man's hat,
          불량배 중 한 명이   그의 모자를 낚아채자,

/ on which he raised his stick / to defend himself and, /
          그는 지팡이를 들어   자신을 지키려고,

swinging it over his head, / smashed the shop window /
머리 위로 휘두르다가,   가게 유리창을 깨고 말았지

behind him. Peterson had rushed forward / to protect the
그의 뒤에 있던.   피터슨이 달려갔지만   그를 도와주려고

stranger / from his assailants; / but the man, / shocked
불량배에게서;   하지만 그 남자는,

at having broken the window, / and seeing an official-
유리창이 깨진 걸 보고 놀란 데다,   제복을 입은 사람이

looking person in uniform / rushing towards him, /
          자신에게 달려오는 것을 보자,

dropped his goose, / took to his heels, / and vanished /
거위를 떨어뜨리고,   달아나더니,   사라져 버렸네

amid the labyrinth of small streets / which lie at the back
미로같은 좁은 골목으로   토튼햄 코트 로드 뒷편에 있는.

of Tottenham Court Road. The roughs had also fled /
          불량배 또한 달아났고

at the appearance of Peterson, / so that he was left / in
피터슨의 모습을 보고,   그래서 피터슨이 남겨진 거지

possession of the field of battle, / and also of the spoils
싸움터를 점령한 채,   승리의 전리품과 함께

of victory / in the shape of this battered hat / and a most
          이 낡은 모자와

unimpeachable Christmas goose."
아무 죄 없는 크리스마스 거위라는."

---

trophy 트로피, 전리품 | battered 낡은 | billycock 중절모자 | in company with ~와 함께 | jollification
흥청망청 놀기, 환락 | stagger 비틀거림 | row 말다툼, 소란 | knot 무리 | rough 불량배 | assailant 폭행범 |
labyrinth 미로 | unimpeachable 의심할 여지없는, 비난할 점이 없는

"Which surely he restored to their owner?"
"거위는 분명 주인에게 돌려 줬겠지?"

"My dear fellow, / there lies the problem. It is true / that
"그런데, 그게 문제가 있네. 사실은

'For Mrs. Henry Baker' was printed / upon a small card
'헨리 베이커 부인에게' 라는 글이 있었네 작은 카드에

/ which was tied to the bird's left leg, / and it is also true
거위 왼발에 묶여 있는, 또 사실은

/ that the initials 'H. B.' are legible / upon the lining of
'H. B.' 라는 이니셜이 써 있었지 이 모자의 안감에,

this hat, / but as there are some thousands of Bakers,
하지만 수천 명의 베이커 씨가 있고,

/ and some hundreds of Henry Bakers / in this city of
헨리 베이커라는 이름도 수백 명이나 되니까 이 도시에는,

ours, / it is not easy / to restore lost property / to any one
쉬운 일이 아니지 잃어버린 물건을 돌려 주는가가 그 중 누구에게."

of them."
그 중 누구에게."

"What, then, did Peterson do?"
"그럼, 피터슨은 어떻게 했지?"

Key Expression

of + 추상명사 = 형용사

영어에서 'of + 추상명사' 는 종종 형용사와 같은 역할을 합니다.
또한 of와 추상명사 사이에 no, little, much, great처럼 정도를 나타내는
형용사를 넣어 표현할 수도 있습니다.

▶ of interest = interesting(흥미로운)
  of importance = important(중요한)
  of consequence = consequent(중요한)
  of use = useful(유용한)
  of value = valuable(가치 있는)

ex) knowing that even the smallest problems are of interest to me.
  아무리 사소한 문제라도 내겐 흥미롭다는 사실을 알고서.
  It would have been of no use to anyone had we not done so.
  우리가 그렇게 하지 않았다면 그건 상해 버려 아무에게도 쓸모 없게 되었을 겁니다.
  It is a matter of no importance;
  그건 전혀 중요한 문제가 아니야.

"He brought round / both hat and goose / to me / on
"그는 가져왔네   모자와 거위 모두를   내게

Christmas morning, / knowing / that even the smallest
크리스마스 날 아침에,   알고서   아무리 사소한 문제라도

problems are / of interest to me. The goose / we retained
내가 흥미로워한다는 사실을. 거위는   우리가 갖고 있었는데

/ until this morning, / when there were signs that, / in
오늘 아침까지,   조짐이 보여서,

spite of the slight frost, / it would be well that it should
추운 날씨에도,   먹어 버리는 게 좋겠다는

be eaten / without unnecessary delay. Its finder has
지체하지 않고.   발견한 사람이 가지고 갔지,

carried it off, / therefore, / to fulfil the ultimate destiny
그래서,   거위의 궁극적인 운명을 완수할 수 있도록,

of a goose, / while I continue to retain / the hat of the
하지만 계속 간직하고 있네   이름 모를 신사의 모자는

unknown gentleman / who lost his Christmas dinner."
크리스마스 만찬을 잃어버린."

"Did he not advertise?"
"주인이 분실 광고를 내진 않았나?"

"No."
"아니."

"Then, / what clue could you have / as to his identity?"
"그럼,   어떤 단서가 있는 거지   그의 신원을 알아낼?"

"Only as much as we can deduce."
"추리할 수 있는 게 전부지."

"From his hat?"
"모자로?"

"Precisely."
"맞았어."

"But you are joking. What can you gather / from this old
"농담이겠지.   뭘 알아낼 수 있다는 건가

battered felt?"
이 낡고 망가진 모자에서?"

destiny 운명 | deduce 추론하다

97

"Here is my lens. You know my methods. What can you
"여기 돋보기가 있네. 자네는 내 방식을 알고 있지. 자네가 직접 뭘 알아낼

gather yourself / as to the individuality of the man / who
수 있겠나 사람의 신원에 대해서

has worn this article?"
이 모자를 썼던?"

I took the tattered object / in my hands / and turned it
나는 낡은 모자를 집어 들고 두 손으로 뒤집어 보았다

over / rather ruefully. It was a very ordinary black hat /
다소 측은해하며. 매우 평범한 검은 모자였다

of the usual round shape, / hard and much the worse for
둥근 태의, 쓰고 다니기에는 너무 낡은.

wear. The lining had been of red silk, / but was a good
안감에 빨간 비단을 댔지만, 색이 많이 바래 있었다.

deal discoloured. There was no maker's name; / but,
만든 사람의 이름은 없었지만; 그러나,

/ as Holmes had remarked, / the initials "H. B." were
홈즈가 말한 대로 'H. B.' 라는 이니셜이 휘갈겨 쓰여 있었다

scrawled / upon one side. It was pierced / in the brim /
한 쪽에. 구멍이 뚫려 있었는데 챙에는

for a hat-securer, / but the elastic was missing. For the
끈을 끼울 수 있도록, 고무 밴드가 없었다. 나머지 부분은,

rest, / it was cracked, / exceedingly dusty, / and spotted
갈라져 있었고, 먼지가 수북하게 앉아 있었으며,

in several places, / although there seemed to have been
군데군데 얼룩이 져 있었다. 시도한 듯 보였지만

some attempt / to hide the discoloured patches / by
변색된 부분을 감추려고

smearing them with ink.
잉크를 칠해서.

"I can see nothing," / said I, / handing it back to my
"전혀 모르겠는데," 내가 말했다, 친구에게 모자를 다시 돌려 주며.

friend.

"On the contrary, / Watson, / you can see everything.
"반대로, 왓슨, 자넨 모든 걸 보았네.

You fail, / however, / to reason from what you see. You
실패한 거지, 하지만 자네가 본 걸 바탕으로 추리하는 데. 자네는

are too timid / in drawing your inferences."
지나치게 소심하군 추리를 이끌어내는 데."

"Then, / pray tell me / what it is / that you can infer /
"그럼, 말해 보게 도대체 뭘 추리할 수 있는지

from this hat?"
이 모자에서?"

He picked it up / and gazed at it / in the peculiar
그는 모자를 집어들더니 응시했다 특유의 성찰하는 듯한 태도로

introspective fashion / which was characteristic of him.
그의 특징적인 버릇대로.

---

tattered 낡은, 다 망가진 | ruefully 가련하게 | scrawl 휘갈겨 쓰다, 낙서를 하다 | brim 모자의 챙 | elastic
고무 밴드 | patche 부분 | introspective 자기 성찰적인

"It is perhaps less suggestive / than it might have been,"
"연상되는 게 적을지도 모르겠군   예상했던 것보다,"

/ he remarked, / "and yet / there are a few inferences
그가 말했다.   "하지만   몇 가지 추리할 수 있어

/ which are very distinct, / and a few others / which
매우 분명한 사실을,   그리고 몇 가지 더 있네

represent / at least / a strong balance of probability. That
보여 주는 게   적어도   가능성이 매우 높은 사실을.

the man was highly intellectual / is of course obvious /
그 남자는 매우 지적인 사람이라는 점은   물론 틀림없네

upon the face of it, / and also that he was fairly well-to-
모자를 보면,   또한 부유하게 살았지만

do / within the last three years, / although he has now
3년 전 쯤에는,   하지만 지금은 불운을 겪고 있군.

fallen upon evil days. He had foresight, / but has less
선견지명이 있었지만,   지금은 예전보다 못하고,

now than formerly, / pointing to a moral retrogression,
정신적으로도 약해졌는데,

/ which, / when taken with the decline of his fortunes, /
그건,   재산을 잃게 되었을 때,

seems to indicate some evil influence, / probably drink,
좋지 않은 영향을 미친 것 같아,   아마도 술이,

/ at work upon him. This may account also for / the
그에게 영향을 미친 거겠지.   또한 이것으로 설명할 수 있지

obvious fact / that his wife has ceased to love him."
분명한 사실도   부인이 그를 사랑하지 않는다는 것도."

"My dear Holmes!"
"여보게 홈즈!"

"He has, / however, / retained some degree of self-
"그는,   하지만,   어느 정도 자존심은 가지고 있어서,"

respect," / he continued, / disregarding my remonstrance.
그가 말을 이었다,   내 항의를 무시하며.

---

inference 추론 | fall on evil days 불운을 겪다 | foresight 예지력, 선견지명 | retrogression 후퇴 |
disregard 무시하다 | remonstrance 항의 | sedentary 주로 앉아서 지내는, 몸을 많이 움직이지 않는 | out of
training 건강이 좋지 않은 | grizzled 반백이 된 | anoint 바르다 | patent 뻔한, 명백한 | improbable 있을 것
같지 않은 | attain 획득하다 | clap 재빨리 놓다

"He is a man who leads a sedentary life, / goes out
그는 잘 돌아다니지 않는 생활을 한 사람이야,   외출도 거의 안하고,

little, / is out of training entirely, / is middle-aged, / has
건강도 좋지 않으며,   중년의 나이에,

grizzled hair / which he has had cut / within the last few
머리가 하얗게 샜는데   머리를 깎았고   지난 며칠 사이에,

days, / and which he anoints with lime-cream. These are
라임 크림을 바르지.

the more patent facts / which are to be deduced from his
이 정도가 좀 더 명백한 사실들이지   이 모자에서 추리해 낼 수 있는.

hat. Also, / by the way, / that it is extremely improbable /
또한,   그런데,   가능성이 매우 높아

that he has gas laid / on in his house."
가스등을 설치하지 않았을   자신의 집에."

"You are certainly joking, / Holmes."
"자네 농담하는 거지,   홈즈."

"Not in the least. Is it possible / that even now, / when I
"전혀.   아마도   이제는,   내가 자네에게

give you these results, / you are unable to see / how they
추리 결과를 이야기 했으니,   자네도 알 수 있겠지

are attained?"
어떻게 그런 결과가 나왔는지?"

"I have no doubt / that I am very stupid, / but I must
"틀림없이   내가 아주 바보인가보군,   하지만 고백해야겠네

confess / that I am unable to follow you. For example, /
자네 말을 이해할 수 없다고.   예를 들어,

how did you deduce / that this man was intellectual?"
어떻게 추리했나   이 남자가 지적이라고?"

For answer / Holmes clapped the hat / upon his head.
대답으로   홈즈는 모자를 푹 둘러썼다   머리 위에.

It came right over the forehead / and settled upon the
모자는 이마를 지나   콧등에서 멈췄다.

bridge of his nose.

"It is a question of cubic capacity," / said he; / "a man
"그건 부피의 문제야,"   그가 말했다;   "머리가 이렇게

with so large a brain / must have something in it."
큰 사람이라면   그 안에 뭔가 들어있는 게 틀림없지."

"The decline of his fortunes, / then?"
"재산이 줄었다는 건,   그러면?"

"This hat is three years old. These flat brims / curled
"이 모자는 3년 된 거야.   이렇게 챙이 평평하고   끝이 말린 모자는

at the edge / came in then. It is a hat of the very best
그때 유행했지.   이건 최고급 모자네.

quality. Look at the band of ribbed silk and the excellent
골이 지게 짠 비단 챙과 훌륭한 안감을 봐.

lining. If this man could afford to buy / so expensive a
이 남자가 살 수 있었는데   이렇게 비싼 모자를

hat / three years ago, / and has had no hat since, / then /
3년 전에,   그 후에 새 모자가 없었다면,   그때

he has assuredly gone down in the world."
분명 형편이 어려워진 거겠지."

Key Expression

such와 so

such와 so는 둘 다 '그토록, 그 정도의'의 의미로 형용사를 강조하는 비슷한 의미를 가지고 있습니다.
하지만 such는 형용사, so는 부사로 어순에서 차이가 있습니다.

▶ such +부정관사 + 형용사 + 명사
▶ so + 형용사 + 부정관사 + 명사

ex) A man with so large a brain must have something in it.
　　머리가 이렇게 큰 사람이라면 그 안에 뭔가 들어있는 게 틀림없지.
　　If this man could afford to buy so expensive a hat three years ago…
　　이 남자가 3년 전에 이렇게 비싼 모자를 살 수 있었다면…
　　When your wife allows you to go out in such a state…
　　자네 부인이 자네가 그런 모습으로 나가도록 놔 둘 때는…

"Well, / that is clear enough, / certainly. But how about
"음,　　확실히 그렇군,　　　　　분명히.

the foresight and the moral retrogression?"
하지만 통찰력과 정신적으로 나약해졌다는 것은?"

Sherlock Holmes laughed.
셜록 홈즈는 웃음을 터뜨렸다.

"Here is the foresight," / said he / putting his finger /
"이게 바로 통찰력이네,"　　　그가 말했다　손가락으로 가리키며

upon the little disc and loop of the hat-securer.
모자 끈을 끼우는 작은 구멍을.

"They are never sold upon hats. If this man ordered one,
"모자에 구멍을 낸 채 팔지는 않네.　　　이 남자가 그런 모자를 주문했다면,

/ it is a sign of a certain amount of foresight, / since he
그건 꽤 통찰력이 있다는 뜻이지,　　　　왜냐하면 그는

went out of his way / to take this precaution / against the
특별히 노력한 것이니까　이렇게 대비하려고　　　바람에 날려가지

wind. But since we see / that he has broken the elastic
않도록.　하지만 보이니까　고무끈이 끊어졌는데

/ and has not troubled to replace it, / it is obvious / that
바꿔 끼우는 수고를 하지 않은 점이,　　　분명히

he has less foresight now / than formerly, / which is a
이제는 통찰력이 떨어진 것이지　예전보다,

distinct proof / of a weakening nature. On the other
그건 명백한 증거야　정신적으로 나약해졌다는.　오히려,

hand, / he has endeavoured to conceal / some of these
그는 애써 감추려고 했어　　　모자의 얼룩을

stains upon the felt / by daubing them with ink, / which
잉크를 칠해서,

is a sign / that he has not entirely lost his self-respect."
그건 의미하지　그가 자존심을 완전히 잃어버린 것은 아니라고."

"Your reasoning is certainly plausible."
"자네의 추리는 정말 그럴듯 하군."

---

cubic 육적의 | come in 유행하다 | ribbed 골이 지게 짠 | afford to ~할 여유가 있다 | assuredly 분명히,
틀림없이 | go out of one's way 특별히 노력하다 | on the other hand 다른 한편으로는, 반면에 | endeavour
힘껏 노력하다, 분투하다 | conceal 감추다 | daub 바르다 | plausible 그럴듯한

"The further points, / that he is middle-aged, / that his
"더 나아가서, 그가 중년이며,

hair is grizzled, / that it has been recently cut, / and that
머리가 하얗게 세었고, 최근에 깎았다는 점,

he uses lime-cream, / are all to be gathered / from a
그리고 라임 크림을 사용한다는 건, 모두 알게 되었지

close examination / of the lower part of the lining. The
자세히 살펴봐서 안감의 아래쪽을.

lens discloses a large number of hair-ends, / clean cut by
돋보기로 보면 머리 끝이 잔뜩 보이거든,

the scissors of the barber. They all appear to be adhesive,
이발사의 가위로 깔끔하게 잘라낸. 그것이 모두 끈적하게 달라붙어 있고,

/ and there is a distinct odour of lime-cream. This dust,
라임 크림 냄새가 분명히 나지. 이 먼지는,

/ you will observe, / is not the gritty, / grey dust of the
자네도 보이겠지만, 모래같은, 거리의 잿빛 먼지가 아니라,

street / but the fluffy brown dust of the house, / showing
보풀같은 집 안의 갈색 먼지야, 보여 주는

/ that it has been hung up indoors / most of the time, /
모자가 집 안에 걸려 있었다는 것을 대부분,

while the marks of moisture upon the inside / are proof
반면 모자 안쪽의 얼룩은

positive / that the wearer perspired very freely, / and
증거야 모자 주인이 땀을 흘렸다는,

could therefore, / hardly be in the best of training."
그러니, 건강 상태가 좋다고 할 수 없지."

"But his wife / — you said / that she had ceased to love
"하지만 아내 얘기는 — 말했잖아 아내가 그를 사랑하지 않는다고."

him."

"This hat has not been brushed / for weeks. When I see
"이 모자는 솔질을 하지 않았네 몇 주 동안. 내가 자네를 본다면,

you, / my dear Watson, / with a week's accumulation of
왓슨, 몇 주일 동안 먼지가 쌓여 있는데

dust / upon your hat, / and when your wife allows you to
모자 위에.   부인이 자네를 내보낸다면

go out / in such a state, / I shall fear / that you also have
그런 상태로,   생각할 거야   자네 또한 불행히도

been unfortunate / enough to lose your wife's affection."
부인의 사랑을 잃은 것이라고."

"But he might be a bachelor."
"하지만 독신일 수도 있잖나."

"Nay, / he was bringing home the goose / as a peace-
"아니,   그는 거위를 집으로 가져가는 중이었네

offering to his wife. Remember the card / upon the bird's
아내에게 화해의 선물로.   카드를 생각해 보게   거위 발목에 매달린."

leg."

"You have an answer to everything. But how on earth do
"자네는 모든 문제의 답을 찾아내는군.   하지만 도대체 어떻게 추리한 거지

you deduce / that the gas is not laid on / in his house?"
가스등이 설치되지 않았다는 사실을   그의 집에?"

"One tallow stain, / or even two, / might come / by
"수지 얼룩 한 번이나,   혹은 두 번은,   생길 수도 있을 거야

chance; / but when I see no less than five, / I think /
우연히;   하지만 다섯 개 이상이나 보이면,   생각하지

that there can be little doubt / that the individual must
의심할 바 없이   이 사람이 들고 다닌 거라고

be brought into / frequent contact with burning tallow
자주 불 붙은 양초를

/ — walks upstairs at night probably / with his hat in
— 아마도 밤에 계단을 올라가곤 한 거지   한 손에는 모자를 들고

one hand / and a guttering candle in the other. Anyhow,
다른 손에는 타고 있는 양초를 든 채.   어쨌든,

/ he never got tallow-stains / from a gas-jet. Are you
수지 얼룩이 묻었을 리는 없잖아   가스등에서.

satisfied?"
만족했나?"

adhesive 들러붙는 | gritty 모래 같은 | perspire 땀을 흘리다 | accumulation 축적 | tallow 수지(양초나 비누
등을 만드는 데 쓰이는 동물 기름) | bring into ~으로 운반하다 | gutter 촛불이 펄럭거리며 타다

105

"Well, / it is very ingenious," / said I, / laughing; / "but
"흠,　　　그건 아주 기발한데,"　　　　　내가 말했다, 웃으며;　　　　"하지만,

since, / as you said just now, / there has been no crime
방금 전에 자네가 말한 대로,　　　　범죄가 일어나지 않았고,

committed, / and no harm done / save the loss of a goose,
피해도 없다면　　　　　　　거위를 잃어버린 것 외에,

/ all this seems to be rather a waste of energy."
이 모든 추리가 헛수고가 될 것 같은데."

Sherlock Holmes had opened his mouth to reply, / when
셜록 홈즈가 대답하려고 입을 열려는데,

the door flew open, / and Peterson, / the commissionaire,
그때 문이 활짝 열리더니,　　　피터슨이,　　　　　수위인,

/ rushed into the apartment / with flushed cheeks / and
뛰어 들어왔다　　　　　　　볼이 상기된 채

the face of a man / who is dazed with astonishment.
그리고 그의 얼굴은　　　놀라서 멍한 상태였다.

"The goose, / Mr. Holmes! The goose, sir!" / he gasped.
"거위가, 홈즈 씨! 거위가요!" 그는 숨을 헐떡였다.

"Eh? What of it, then? Has it returned to life / and
"뭐? 거위가 왜? 거위가 살아나서 날아가

flapped off / through the kitchen window?"
버리기라도 했나 부엌 창문으로?"

Holmes twisted himself round / upon the sofa / to get a
홈즈는 몸을 틀어 소파 위에서

fairer view / of the man's excited face.
똑바로 바라보았다 남자의 흥분한 얼굴을.

"See here, sir! See what my wife found / in its crop!"
"이걸 보세요, 선생님! 아내가 찾아낸 것을 보세요 모이주머니 속에서!"

He held out his hand / and displayed / upon the centre of
그는 손을 내밀어 보여 주었다 손바닥 가운데에서

the palm / a brilliantly scintillating blue stone, / rather
눈부시게 빛나는 푸른 보석을,

smaller than a bean in size, / but of such purity and
크기는 콩알보다 좀 작았지만, 순도와 광채가 무척 뛰어나

radiance / that it twinkled / like an electric point / in the
반짝였다 마치 전등을 켠 듯이

dark hollow of his hand.
손바닥의 어두운 홈에서.

Sherlock Holmes sat up / with a whistle.
셜록 홈즈는 똑바로 앉아 휘파람을 불었다.

"By Jove, / Peterson!" / said he, / "this is treasure trove
"이런, 피터슨!" 그가 말했다, "이건 정말 귀중한 보물이군.

indeed. I suppose you know / what you have got?"
자네도 알 것 같은데 뭘 발견한 건지?"

"A diamond, sir? A precious stone. It cuts into glass / as
"다이아몬드인가요? 보석이죠. 이걸로 유리를 자르지요

though it were putty."
퍼티처럼."

---

ingenious 기발한 | dazed 멍한 | flap 날개를 퍼덕이며 날다 | crop (조류의) 모이주머니 | scintillating 반짝반짝
빛나는 | radiance 빛, 광채 | by Jove 어이쿠, 저런 | trove 발견물 귀중한 수집물; 획득물 | putty 퍼티(유리를
창틀에 끼울 때 바르는 접합제)

107

"It's more than a precious stone. It is the precious stone."
"이건 보석보다 더 귀한 거라네.　　　　　　하나밖에 없는 보석이지."

"Not the Countess of Morcar's blue carbuncle!" / I
"모르카 백작부인의 푸른 카벙클이 아닌가!"

ejaculated.
내가 갑자기 소리쳤다.

"Precisely so. I ought to know its size and shape, / seeing
"맞아.　　　　크기와 모양이 이 정도일 줄은 몰랐네,

that I have read the advertisement about it / in The
광고에서 읽었는데　　　　　　　　　〈타임즈〉에 게재된

Times / every day lately. It is absolutely unique, / and its
최근 날마다.　　　　　이건 하나밖에 없는 것이고,

value can only be conjectured, / but the reward offered
가치는 짐작할 수밖에 없지만,　　　　현상금으로 내건 1,000파운드는

of £1000 / is certainly not within a twentieth part of the
분명히 시장 가격의 20분의 1도 안 될 거야."

market price."

"A thousand pounds! Great Lord of mercy!"
"1,000파운드라고요!　　　　자비로우신 주여!"

The commissionaire plumped down / into a chair / and
수위는 털썩 주저 앉아　　　　　　　의자에

stared / from one to the other of us.
바라보았다　우리 둘을 번갈아.

"That is the reward, / and I have reason to know / that
"현상금은 그렇지,　　　　그런데 내가 알기론

there are sentimental considerations / in the background
감정적인 이유가 있는 것 같아　　　　　　그 배경에는

/ which would induce / the Countess to part with half her
추리해 보면　　　　　　백작 부인이 재산의 절반이라도 주겠다고 한 것으로

fortune / if she could but recover the gem."
보석을 되찾을 수만 있다면."

ejaculate 갑자기 외치다 | conjecture 추측하다 | plump 털썩 떨어지다 | sentimental 감정적인 | part with
~을 주다 | gem 보석 | abstract 추출하다, 끝내다 | refer to 맡기다, 회부하다 | assizes (예전 잉글랜드·
웨일스의) 순회 재판소

"It was lost, / if I remember aright, / at the Hotel
"잃어버렸지,　　　내 기억이 맞다면,

Cosmopolitan," / I remarked.
코스모폴리탄 호텔에서,"　　내가 말했다.

"Precisely so, / on December 22nd, / just five days
"맞네,　　　　　12월 22일에,　　　　바로 닷새 전이지.

ago. John Horner, / a plumber, / was accused of having
존 호너가,　　　　배관공인,　　그걸 훔쳐냈다고 혐의를 받고 있지

abstracted it / from the lady's jewel-case. The evidence
부인의 보석함에서.

against him was so strong / that the case has been
그에 대한 증거가 확실해서　　　사건은 순회재판에 회부되었지.

referred to the Assizes. I have some account of the
그 사건에 대한 설명이 여기 있을텐데,

matter here, / I believe."
내 생각엔."

He rummaged amid his newspapers, / glancing over the
그는 신문을 뒤적거리더니,   날짜를 살피면서,

dates, / until at last / he smoothed one out, / doubled it
마침내   한 장을 꺼내어 펴서,   반으로 접어,

over, / and read the following paragraph: /
다음의 내용을 읽었다:

"Hotel Cosmopolitan Jewel Robbery. John Horner, 26,
"코스모폴리탄 호텔 보석 도난 사건.   26세의 배관공 존 호너가,

plumber, / was brought up upon the charge of having /
혐의를 받고 기소되었다

upon the 22nd inst., / abstracted from the jewel-case of
이달 22일에,   모르카 백작 부인의 보석함에서 훔쳤다는

the Countess of Morcar / the valuable gem / known as
귀금속을

the blue carbuncle. James Ryder, / upper-attendant at
푸른 카벙클이라고 알려진.   제임스 라이더가,   호텔 지배인인,

the hotel, / gave his evidence / to the effect that he had
증언했다   자신이 호너를 데려갔다는 내용으로

shown Horner up / to the dressing-room of the Countess
모르카 백작 부인의 드레스룸으로

of Morcar / upon the day of the robbery / in order that he
도난 사건이 일어난 날에   납땜하기 위해

might solder / the second bar of the grate, / which was
난로의 두번째 쇠살대를   헐거워진.

loose. He had remained with Horner / some little time,
그는 호너와 함께 있었지만   잠시 동안,

/ but had finally been called away. On returning, / he
호출을 받고 떠났다.   돌아왔을 때,

found / that Horner had disappeared, / that the bureau
발견했다   호너는 사라져 버렸고,

had been forced open, / and that the small morocco
서랍장이 강제로 열려 있었으며,   작은 모로코 가죽함은

casket / in which, / as it afterwards transpired, / the
그 안에, 나중에 밝혀진 바에 의하면,

Countess was accustomed to keep her jewel, / was
백작 부인이 보석을 보관했던,

lying empty / upon the dressing-table. Ryder instantly
열려진 채 화장대 위에 놓여 있는 모습을. 라이더는 즉시 신고를 했고,

gave the alarm, / and Horner was arrested / the same
호너는 체포되었다 그날 저녁;

evening; / but the stone could not be found / either upon
하지만 보석은 발견되지 않았다 그의 수중에서도

his person / or in his rooms. Catherine Cusack, / maid
방에서도. 캐서린 쿠삭은,

to the Countess, / deposed / to having heard Ryder's cry
백작 부인의 하녀인, 증언했다 라이더가 지른 비명을 듣고

of dismay / on discovering the robbery, / and to having
도난 현장을 보고 놀라서, 방 안으로 달려가

rushed into the room, / where she found matters / as
현장을 보았다고 했다

described by the last witness. Inspector Bradstreet, / B
라이더가 진술한 대로의. 브레드스트리트 경위는,

division, / gave evidence / as to the arrest of Horner, /
B지구대의, 증언했다 호너를 체포할 때,

who struggled frantically, / and protested his innocence /
그가 미친 듯이 저항하며, 자신의 결백을 주장했다고

in the strongest terms. Evidence of a previous conviction
강한 어조로. 절도 전과가 밝혀지자

for robbery / having been given against the prisoner,
피의자에게 있었던,

/ the magistrate refused to deal summarily / with the
치안판사는 즉결재판을 거부하고, 그 사건에 대해,

offence, / but referred it to the Assizes.
순회재판에 회부했다.

---

rummage 뒤지다 | amid 가운데 | smooth out 주름을 펴다 | inst. 이달, 금월 | to the effect ~이라는 의미의
| solder 납땜하다 | bureau 옷장 서랍 | depose 증언하다 | dismay 실망, 경악 | frantically 미친 듯이, 몹시 |
protest 항의하다, 이의를 제기하다 | conviction 유죄 선고 | magistrate 치안 판사 | deal summarily 즉결로
처리하다

Horner, / who had shown signs of intense emotion /
호너는,　　　격한 감정을 보이다가

during the proceedings, / fainted away / at the conclusion
심리가 진행되는 동안,　　　　　기절하여　　　　판결이 끝나자

/ and was carried out of court."
법정 밖으로 실려 나갔다."

"Hum! So much for the police-court," / said Holmes /
"음!　　즉결 재판에 대해선 그 정도로 하고,"　　　홈즈가 말했다

thoughtfully, / tossing aside the paper.
생각에 잠긴 듯 ,　　　신문을 한쪽으로 던지며.

Key Expression

nothing but = only

nothing but에서 but은 '~이외에는'이란 의미로, nothing but은 '이외에는 아무것도', 즉 '단지 ~밖에, ~뿐'의 뜻의 숙어입니다. 즉 only와 같은 의미로 볼 수 있습니다.
비슷한 형태의 anything but은 '결코 ~가 아닌' (=never)라는 뜻의 전혀 다른 숙어이니 혼동하지 않도록 주의하세요.

ex) He was clearly so scared by his mischance in breaking the window and by
the approach of Peterson that he thought of nothing but flight.
그는 실수로 창문을 깨뜨린 데다가 피터슨이 다가오는 것을 보고 너무 놀라서
도망칠 생각밖에 못한 게 분명해.

"The question for us now to solve / is the sequence of
"지금 우리가 풀어야 할 문제는   일련의 사건들이지

events / leading from a rifled jewel-case / at one end /
도난 당한 보석함에서 시작해   한 쪽에선

to the crop of a goose / in Tottenham Court Road / at
거위의 모이주머니에 이어지는   토튼햄 코트 로드의

the other. You see, / Watson, / our little deductions /
다른 한쪽에선. 알겠지만,   왓슨,   우리의 사소한 추리가

have suddenly assumed / a much more important / and
갑자기 특징을 띠게 되었네   훨씬 더 중요하고

less innocent aspect. Here is the stone; / the stone came
무죄 가능성이 희박해진 양상으로. 여기 보석이 있네;

from the goose, / and the goose came from Mr. Henry
보석은 거위로부터 나왔고,   거위는 헨리 베이커 씨의 것인데,

Baker, / the gentleman with the bad hat / and all the
        그 신사는 낡은 모자를 썼고

other characteristics / with which I have bored you. So
특징을 가진 인물이지   내가 자네에게 길게 떠들어 댄.   그러니

now / we must set ourselves very seriously / to finding
이제   우리는 아주 진지하게 시작해야 하네

this gentleman / and ascertaining / what part he has
이 신사를 찾아서   확인해야지   그가 어떤 역할을 했는지

played / in this little mystery. To do this, / we must try
        이 사건에서.   그러기 위해선,

the simplest means first, / and these lie undoubtedly / in
가장 간단한 방법부터 시도해야 하는데,   그건 분명

an advertisement / in all the evening papers. If this fail, /
광고를 내는 것이야   모든 석간 신문에.   이 방법이 실패하면,

I shall have recourse to other methods."
다른 방법을 찾아봐야겠지."

"What will you say?"
"뭐라고 할 건데?"

---

so much for ~은 그 정도로 하고 | rifle 훔치다 | assume 특징을 띠다 | bored (말을 너무 많이 해서) 지루하게
만들다 | ascertain 확인하다 | have recourse to ~을 사용하다

113

"Give me a pencil and that slip of paper. Now, / then: /
"연필과 종이 좀 주게. 자, 그럼:

'Found at the corner of Goodge Street, / a goose and a
'구지 가 모퉁이에서 발견, 거위 한 마리와 검은색

black felt hat. Mr. Henry Baker can have the same by
펠트 모자를. 헨리 베이커 씨는 이상의 것을 찾아가시길

applying / at 6.30 this evening / at 221b, Baker Street.'
오늘 저녁 6시 30분에 베이커 가 221b번지에서.'

That is clear and concise."
이 정도면 간단명료하지."

"Very. But will he see it?"
"그렇군. 그런데 그가 볼까?"

"Well, / he is sure to keep an eye on the papers, / since, /
"음, 그는 틀림없이 신문을 살피고 있을 거야, 왜냐하면,

to a poor man, / the loss was a heavy one. He was clearly
가난한 사람에게, 큰 손실이었으니까. 분명히 너무 놀라서

so scared / by his mischance / in breaking the window
실수로 창문을 깨뜨린 데다가

/ and by the approach of Peterson / that he thought of
피터슨이 다가오는 것을 보고 도망칠 생각밖에 못한 거야,

nothing but flight, / but since then / he must have bitterly
하지만 그때 이후로 심하게 후회하고 있을 거야

regretted / the impulse which caused him to drop his
충동적으로 거위를 떨어뜨린 것에 대해.

bird. Then, / again, / the introduction of his name / will
그러니, 다시 한 번, 자신의 이름이 나오면

cause him to see it, / for everyone who knows him / will
볼 수밖에 없겠지, 왜냐하면 그를 아는 모든 사람들이

direct his attention to it. Here you are, / Peterson, / run
그에게 알려 줄 테니. 여기 있네, 피터슨,

down to the advertising agency / and have this put in the
광고 대행사로 달려가서 이걸 석간 신문에 싣도록 하게."

evening papers."

---

keep an eye on ~을 계속 지켜보다 | impulse 충동 | agency 대행사

"In which, sir?"
"어느 신문에요?"

"Oh, in the Globe, / Star, / Pall Mall, / St. James's, /
"아, 글로브, 스타, 펠 멜, 세인트제임스,

Evening News, / Standard, / Echo, / and any others / that
이브닝 뉴스, 스탠더드, 에코에, 그리고 다른 신문에도

occur to you."
생각나는 대로."

"Very well, sir. And this stone?"
"알겠습니다. 그럼 이 보석은요?"

"Ah, yes, / I shall keep the stone. Thank you. And, / I
"아, 그렇군, 보석은 내가 보관하겠네. 고맙네. 그리고,

say, Peterson, / just buy a goose / on your way back / and
저기, 피터슨, 거위 한 마리만 사서 돌아오는 길에

leave it here with me, / for we must have one / to give to
내게 갖다주게, 한 마리 갖고 있어야 하니

this gentleman / in place of the one / which your family /
이 남자에게 줄 그 거위 대신 자네 가족이

is now devouring."
지금 먹어치우고 있는."

When the commissionaire had gone, / Holmes took up
수위가 떠나자 홈즈는 보석을 들고

the stone / and held it against the light.
빛에 비춰 보았다.

"It's a bonny thing," / said he.
"정말 아름답군," 그가 말했다.

"Just see how it glints and sparkles. Of course / it is a
"얼마나 빛나고 반짝거리는지 좀 보게. 물론

nucleus and focus of crime. Every good stone is. They
이게 범죄의 핵심이자 표적이겠지. 모든 보석은 그래.

are the devil's pet baits. In the larger and older jewels /
보석은 악마가 쓰는 미끼지. 보석이 크고 오래될수록

every facet may stand / for a bloody deed. This stone is
그 모든 단면은 상징하고 있는 거야 피로 얼룩진 유혈극을.

not yet twenty years old. It was found / in the banks of
이 보석은 20년도 채 안 됐지.　　　발견되었는데　　　아모이 강 제방에서

the Amoy River / in southern China / and is remarkable
　　　　　　　중국 남부의　　　주목할 만하지

/ in having every characteristic of the carbuncle, / save
카벙클의 모든 특징을 지녔다는 점에서,　　　　　푸른 색이

that it is blue / in shade instead of ruby red. In spite of
라는 점을 제외하곤　　루비같은 붉은 색이 아니라.　　발견된 지 얼마

its youth, / it has already a sinister history. There have
안 됐지만,　이 보석은 이미 불길한 역사를 지니고 있어.

been two murders, / a vitriol-throwing, / a suicide, / and
두 건의 살인 사건이 있었고,　황산 투척,　　자살,

several robberies brought about / for the sake of this
그리고 여러 건의 도난 사건이 일어났어

forty-*grain weight of crystallised charcoal. Who would
이 40그레인의 무게를 지닌 탄소결정체를 두고.　　　누가 생각하겠나

think / that so pretty a toy would be a purveyor / to the
　　이렇게 예쁜 장난감이 거점이 될 거라고

gallows and the prison? I'll lock it up in my strong box
교수대와 감옥으로 향하는?　　이것을 내 금고에 넣어 잠궈 두고

/ now / and drop a line to the Countess / to say that we
이제　　백작 부인에게 서신을 보내야겠군　　우리가 이걸 갖고 있다고."

have it."

"Do you think that this man Horner is innocent?"
"호너라는 자는 무죄라고 생각하나?"

"I cannot tell."
"알 수 없지."

"Well, then, / do you imagine / that this other one, /
"음, 그렇다면,　자네 생각에는　　다른 남자인,

Henry Baker, / had anything to do with the matter?"
헨리 베이커가,　이 사건과 관계가 있다는 건가?"

* 그레인은 아주 적은 양을 나타내는 무게의 단위. 당시 영국의 보석 1캐럿은 약 3.1687그레인으로,
40그레인은 12.62캐럿이다.

I say 제[여보세요/있잖아요](상대방의 관심을 끌거나 새로운 화제를 도입할 때 씀) | devour 걸신 들린 듯 먹다 |
bonny 어여쁜 | glint 반짝임 | nucleus 핵, 핵심 | bait 미끼 | facet 측면 | sinister 사악한, 불길한 | vitriol
황산 | crystallised 결정체의 | purveyor 공급업자 | gallows 교수대

"It is, / I think, / much more likely / that Henry Baker
"그건,　내 생각에　가능성이 높아

is an absolutely innocent man, / who had no idea / that
헨리 베이커는 전혀 죄가 없다는 데,　그는 아무것도 모르지

the bird which he was carrying / was of considerably
자신이 들고 가던 거위가　훨씬 값나가는 물건이란 걸

more value / than if it were made of solid gold. That, /
그게 금으로 만든 것이라 하더라도.　그건,

however, / I shall determine / by a very simple test / if
하지만,　결정할 거야　간단한 테스트로

we have an answer to our advertisement."
우리 광고에 대한 답변이 오면."

"And can you do nothing / until then?"
"그럼 아무것도 할 수 없는 건가　그때까진?"

"Nothing."
"아무것도."

"In that case / I shall continue my professional round.
"그렇다면　나는 일을 좀 해야겠군.

But I shall come back / in the evening / at the hour you
하지만 돌아올 거야　저녁 때　자네가 말한 시간까지는,

have mentioned, / for I should like to see / the solution of
나도 보고 싶으니까

so tangled a business."
이토록 복잡하게 얽힌 사건이 해결되는 모습을."

"Very glad to see you. I dine at seven. There is a
"자네를 보면 반가울 거야.　저녁 식사는 7시야.　누른도요새 요리가 있을 거야,

woodcock, / I believe. By the way, / in view of recent
내 생각엔.　그건 그렇고,　좀 전에 일어난 일을 생각해서,

occurrences, / perhaps I ought to ask Mrs. Hudson / to
허드슨 부인에게 부탁해야겠군

examine its crop."
새의 모이주머니를 잘 살피라고."

---

tangled 얽혀 있는 | dine 식사를 하다, 만찬을 들다 | woodcock 누른도요새

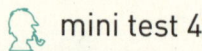 mini test 4

A. 다음 문장을 해석해 보세요.

(1) Amid the action and reaction / of so dense a swarm of
humanity, / every possible combination of events / may be
expected to take place, / and many a little problem / will be
presented / which may be striking and bizarre / without being
criminal.
→

(2) The roughs had also fled / at the appearance of Peterson, /
so that he was left / in possession of the field of battle, / and
also of the spoils of victory / in the shape of this battered hat
/ and a most unimpeachable Christmas goose.
→

(3) There has been no crime committed, / and no harm done /
save the loss of a goose, / all this seems to be rather a waste
of energy.
→

(4) The question for us now to solve / is the sequence of events /
leading from a rifled jewel-case / at one end / to the crop of a
goose / in Tottenham Court Road / at the other.
→

B. 다음 주어진 문장이 되도록 빈칸에 써 넣으세요.

(1) 자네가 그걸 낡은 중절모가 아니라 하나의 지적인 문제로써 여겨 주길 바라네.

I beg that you will look upon it _____

_____.

(2) 부인이 그를 사랑하지 않을 거란 분명한 사실도 이것으로 설명할 수 있을 거야.

_____ the obvious fact that his

wife has ceased to love him.

A. (1) 그토록 빽빽하게 모여 있는 인간들의 행동과 반사행동 가운데에서, 범죄가 아니라도 수많은 사건들의
조합이 일어날 수 있고 놀랍고 기괴한 수많은 사소한 문제들이 나타날 것이다. (2) 피터슨의 모습을 보고 불
량배 또한 달아났고, 그래서 그가 싸움터를 점령한 채 이 낡은 모자와 아무 죄 없는 크리스마스 거위라는
승리의 전리품과 함께 남겨진 것이다. (3) 범죄가 일어나지 않았고 거위를 잃어버린 것 외에 피해도 없다면

(3) 우리의 사소한 추리가 갑자기 훨씬 더 중요하고 무죄 가능성이 적은 양상을 띠게 되었네.

Our little deductions have suddenly _____

_____ .

(4) 발견된 지 얼마 안 됐음에도 불구하고, 이 보석은 이미 불길한 역사를 지니고 있어.

_____, it has already a sinister history.

C. 다음 주어진 문구가 알맞은 문장이 되도록 순서를 맞춰 보세요.

(1) 그럴 거라고 예상했던 것보다 연상되는 게 적을지도 모르겠군.
(have / suggestive / might / than / been / it / less)
It is perhaps _____ .

(2) 이 모자로부터 자네가 추리할 수 있는 게 도대체 무엇인가?
(can / What / from / it / you / is / this / hat / that / infer)
→

(3) 즉결 재판에 대해선 그 정도로 하지.
(for / much / the police-court / So)
→

(4) 그는 틀림없이 신문을 살피고 있을 거야.
(the papers / keep / to / He / on / is / an eye / sure)
→

D. 다음 단어에 대한 맞는 설명과 연결해 보세요.

(1) whimsical ▶   ◀ ① damaged or torn

(2) tattered ▶   ◀ ② act of protesting

(3) remonstrance ▶   ◀ ③ likely to be true or valid

(4) plausible ▶   ◀ ④ unusual and unpredictable

Answer

이 모든 추리가 헛수고가 될 것 같다. (4) 지금 우리가 풀어야 할 문제는 한쪽 끝의 도난 당한 보석함으로부터 다른 한쪽 끝의 토트넘 코트 로드에 있는 거위 모이주머니에 이르는 일련의 사건들이다. | B. (1) not as a battered billycock but as an intellectual problem (2) This may account also for (3) assumed a much more important and less innocent aspect (4) In spite of its youth | C. (1) less suggestive than it might have been (2) What is it that you can infer from this hat? (3) So much for the police-court. (4) He is sure to keep an eye on the papers. | D. (1) ④ (2) ① (3) ② (4) ③

2

I had been delayed at a case, / and it was a little after
앞에서 지체되는 바람에,   6시 반이 조금 지난 후였다

half-past six / when I found myself in Baker Street / once
            내가 베이커 가에 돌아간 것은   다시

more. As I approached the house / I saw a tall man / in
한 번. 집 앞에 도착했을 때   키 큰 남자가 보였다

a Scotch bonnet / with a coat / which was buttoned up
모자를 쓰고   코트를 입은 채   단추를 목까지 채운

to his chin / waiting outside / in the bright semicircle /
밖에서 기다리는 모습을   반원형의 불빛 속에서

which was thrown from the fanlight. Just as I arrived /
채광창을 통해 흘러나온.   내가 도착하자마자

the door was opened, / and we were shown up together /
문이 열렸고,   우리는 함께 들어섰다

to Holmes' room.
홈즈의 방에.

"Mr. Henry Baker, / I believe," / said he, / rising from his
"헨리 베이커 씨군요,   제 생각엔,"   그가 말했다,   의자에서 일어나

armchair / and greeting his visitor / with the easy air of
방문객에게 인사하며   편안하고 친절한 태도로

geniality / which he could so readily assume.
그가 마음만 먹으면 취할 수 있는 모습인.

"Pray take this chair by the fire, / Mr. Baker. It is a cold
"난로 옆 이 의자에 앉으세요,   베이커 씨.   날씨가 춥군요,

night, / and I observe / that your circulation is more
제가 보기에   베이커 씨는 여름 날씨에 더 잘 적응하실 것 같네요

adapted for summer / than for winter. Ah, / Watson, /
                   겨울보다는.   아,   왓슨,

you have just come / at the right time. Is that your hat, /
자네도 왔군   때맞춰.   이건 당신 모자인가요,

Mr. Baker?"
베이커 씨?"

---

semicircle 반원 | fanlight 채광창 | geniality 친절 | tremor 떨림 | surmise 추측 | rusty 녹슨, 색이 바랜 |
lank (불룩없게) 죽 뻗은 | protrude 튀어나오다 | staccato 스타카토의 | at a loss 모르는, 당황한

"Yes, / sir, / that is undoubtedly my hat."
"네, 선생님, 틀림없이 제 모자입니다."

He was a large man / with rounded shoulders, / a
그는 체격이 큰 남자로 둥근 어깨,

massive head, / and a broad, intelligent face, / sloping
큰 머리, 넓적하고 지적인 얼굴에,

down to a pointed beard of grizzled brown. A touch
백발이 섞인 갈색의 뾰족한 턱수염을 기른 모습이었다.

of red in nose and cheeks, / with a slight tremor of his
코와 두 뺨은 붉게 물들어 있었고, 내민 손이 약간 떨리고 있어,

extended hand, / recalled Holmes' surmise / as to his
홈즈의 추리가 떠올랐다 그의 습관에 대한.

habits. His rusty black frock-coat was buttoned right up
색이 바랜 검정 프록코트는 단추를 맨 위까지 채우고,

in front, / with the collar turned up, / and his lank wrists
깃을 세웠는데, 가는 손목이 드러나 있었다,

protruded / from his sleeves / without a sign of cuff or
소매 밖으로 셔츠를 입지 않은 듯이.

shirt. He spoke in a slow staccato fashion, / choosing his
그는 느리고 끊어지는 스타카토 같은 말투로 말하고, 조심스럽게 단어를

words with care, / and gave the impression generally of
선택하여, 전체적으로 인상을 주었다

a man of learning / and letters who had had ill-usage / at
학식을 갖춘 사람이라는

the hands of fortune.
불우한 처지에 빠진.

"We have retained these things / for some days," / said
"우리가 이걸 보관하고 있었습니다 며칠 동안,"

Holmes, / "because we expected to see an advertisement
홈즈가 말했다, "광고를 내시길 기다렸거든요

from you / giving your address. I am at a loss to know
주소를 알려 주는. 전혀 모르겠네요

now / why you did not advertise."
왜 광고를 내지 않으셨는지."

Our visitor gave a rather shamefaced laugh.
손님은 다소 무안한 듯 웃었다.

"Shillings have not been so plentiful with me / as they
"돈이 그리 넉넉하지 않아서요

once were," / he remarked.
예전처럼," 그가 말했다.

"I had no doubt / that the gang of roughs / who assaulted
"틀림없이 불량배들이 저를 공격했던

me / had carried off both my hat and the bird. I did not
모자와 거위를 모두 가져간 줄 알았거든요.

care to spend more money / in a hopeless attempt / at
돈을 더 낭비하고 싶지 않았어요 희망이 없는 시도에

recovering them."
그걸 찾으려고."

"Very naturally. By the way, / about the bird, / we were
"그럴 만하군요. 그런데, 거위 말인데,

compelled to eat it."
우리가 먹을 수밖에 없었습니다."

"To eat it!"
"그걸 드셨다고요!"

Our visitor half rose from his chair / in his excitement.
손님은 의자에서 몸을 일으켰다 흥분해서.

"Yes, / it would have been of no use to anyone / had
"네, 상해 버려 아무 쓸모가 없었을 겁니다

we not done so. But I presume / that this other goose
그러지 않았다면. 하지만 제 생각에 다른 거위가 저 찬장에 있는데,

upon the sideboard, / which is about the same weight
같은 무게에 신선한 거위니까,

and perfectly fresh, / will answer your purpose equally
선생님이 의도했던 바에 부합하지 않을까요?"

well?"

---

* 라틴어로 '흩어진 조각' , '절단된 사지', '단편적인 인용구'라는 의미로 쓰이는 말. 로마의 시인 호라티우스의 '풍자시'에 나오는 구절에서 유래했다.

plentiful 풍부한 | be compelled to ~할 수밖에 없다 | presume 추정하다 | fowl (칠면조나 오리 등의) 가금 |
fancier 애호가

"Oh, certainly, certainly," / answered Mr. Baker / with a
"오, 그럼요, 물론입니다," 베이커 씨가 대답했다

sigh of relief.
안도의 한숨을 내쉬며.

"Of course, / we still have the feathers, legs, crop, / and
"물론, 깃털, 다리, 모이주머니는 아직 있습니다,

so on of your own bird, / so if you wish — "
그 거위를 다른 부분도, 그러니 원하신다면 — "

The man burst into a hearty laugh.
남자는 크게 웃음을 터뜨렸다.

"They might be useful to me / as relics of my adventure,"
"그것들도 쓸모가 있겠군요 내가 겪은 모험의 기념품으로,"

/ said he, / "but beyond that / I can hardly see / what
그가 말했다, "하지만 그게 아니라면 모르겠군요

use the *disjecta membra of my late acquaintance
그런 고인이 된 친구의 잘려나간 조각들이

/ are going to be to me. No, sir, / I think that, / with
내게 무슨 소용이 있는지. 아닙니다, 제 생각에,

your permission, / I will confine my attentions / to the
허락해 주신다면, 관심을 두고 싶습니다

excellent bird / which I perceive upon the sideboard."
저 멋진 거위에만 찬장 위에 보이는."

Sherlock Holmes glanced sharply across at me / with a
셜록 홈즈는 재빨리 나를 흘깃 쳐다보았다

slight shrug of his shoulders.
어깨를 으쓱하며.

"There is your hat, / then, / and there your bird," / said
"여기 모자가 있습니다, 그럼, 그리고 거위도요," 그가

he.
말했다.

"By the way, / would it bore you to tell me / where you
"그런데, 알려 주시겠습니까

got the other one from? I am somewhat of a fowl fancier,
예전의 거위를 어디에서 구했는지? 제가 거위를 아주 좋아하는데,

/ and I have seldom seen / a better grown goose."
본 적이 없어서요 그렇게 잘 자란 거위는."

"Certainly, sir," / said Baker, / who had risen / and
"물론이죠," 베이커가 말했다. 자리에서 일어나

tucked his newly gained property / under his arm.
새로 얻은 재산을 끼고서 옆구리에.

"There are a few of us / who frequent the Alpha Inn, /
"사람들이 있습니다 '알파인' 이란 술집에 자주 모이는,

near the Museum / — we are to be found in the Museum
박물관 근처의 — 우린 박물관 안에서 볼 수 있고요

itself / during the day, / you understand. This year
낮 동안에는, 아시겠지만. 올해

/ our good host, / Windigate by name, / instituted a
마음씨 좋은 주인이, '윈디게이트' 라는 이름의, 거위 클럽을 만들었습니다,

goose club, / by which, / on consideration of some few
그 클럽으로, 매주 몇 펜스씩 돈을 내서,

pence every week, / we were each to receive a bird / at
각자 거위 한 마리씩 받기로 했지요

Christmas. My pence were duly paid, / and the rest is
크리스마스에. 저는 제때 돈을 냈고, 나머지 이야기는 선생도

familiar to you. I am much indebted to you, / sir, / for
잘 아시겠지요. 신세 많이 졌습니다, 선생님,

a Scotch bonnet is fitted / neither to my years / nor my
스코틀랜드 모자는 어울리지 않거든요 제 나이에도

gravity."
반백의 머리에도."

With a comical pomposity of manner / he bowed
우스꽝스럽고 과장된 태도로

solemnly to both of us / and strode off upon his way.
그는 우리에게 정중히 인사를 한 뒤 성큼성큼 나가 버렸다.

"So much for Mr. Henry Baker," / said Holmes / when he
"헨리 베이커 씨는 이만하면 됐네," 홈즈가 말했다

had closed the door behind him.
방문을 닫으며.

---

tuck 끼워 넣다 | institute 도입하다 | duly 제때에 | gravity 희끗희끗한 머리 | pomposity 화려, 과장된 언행
| stride 성큼성큼 걷다 | supper 저녁 (하루 끼니 중 마지막에 먹는 것. dinner보다는 덜 격식적이고 규모도 적으며
잠자리에 들기 전에 간단히 먹는 것일 수도 있음)

"It is quite certain / that he knows nothing / whatever
"분명히   그는 아는 게 없군

about the matter. Are you hungry, / Watson?"
사건에 대해선 아무것도.   배고픈가,   왓슨?"

"Not particularly."
"별로."

"Then I suggest / that we turn our dinner into a supper /
"그럼 어떤가   저녁 식사는 밤참으로 미루고

and follow up this clue / while it is still hot."
이 단서를 추적해 보는 게   아직 뜨거울 때."

"By all means."
"좋고 말고."

It was a bitter night, / so we drew on our ulsters / and
몹시 추운 밤이었다,　　　　　　　그래서 우리는 얼스터 외투를 걸치고

wrapped cravats about our throats. Outside, / the stars
스카프를 목에 둘렀다.　　　　　　　　　　　　　밖에는,

were shining coldly / in a cloudless sky, / and the breath
별이 차갑게 빛났고　　　　구름 한 점 없는 하늘에서,

of the passers-by blew out into smoke / like so many
행인들의 입에서는 입김이 흩어져 나왔다　　　　　권총을 마구 쏘아대듯이.

pistol shots. Our footfalls rang out / crisply and loudly /
　　　　　　우리가 내는 발자국 소리는 울려 퍼졌다　또렷하고 크게

as we swung / through the doctors' quarter, / Wimpole
우리가 지나가는 동안　병원가를 통과하여,

Street, / Harley Street, / and so through Wigmore Street
윔폴 가,　　할리 가,　　　　　　　위그모어 가를 지나

/ into Oxford Street. In a quarter of an hour / we were in
　옥스포드 가로 들어설 때까지.　15분 만에

Bloomsbury / at the Alpha Inn, / which is a small public-
우리는 블룸즈베리의　'알파 인'에 도착했는데,　그곳은 작은 선술집이었다

house / at the corner of one of the streets / which runs
　　　　거리 모퉁이에 있는

down into Holborn. Holmes pushed open the door of the
홀본 가로 통하는.　　　홈즈는 술집 문을 밀어 젖혔고

private bar / and ordered two glasses of beer / from the
　　　　　맥주 두 잔을 주문했다

ruddy-faced, / white-aproned landlord.
불그스레한 얼굴의,　흰색 앞치마를 두른 주인에게.

"Your beer should be excellent / if it is as good as your
"맥주 맛이 훌륭겠군요　　　　　　　맥주가 당신네 거위만큼 좋다면,"

geese," / said he.
　　　　홈즈가 말했다.

"My geese!"
"거위라니요!"

ulsters 얼스터 (옛 아일랜드 지방) | cravat 크라바트(넥타이처럼 매는 남성용 스카프)

The man seemed surprised.
주인은 놀란 것 같아 보였다.

"Yes. I was speaking / only half an hour ago / to Mr.
"네. 얘기하고 있었거든요 30분 전에

Henry Baker, / who was a member of your goose club."
헨리 베이커 씨와, 이 집 거위 클럽의 회원이라 하더군요."

"Ah! Yes, I see. But you see, sir, / them's not our geese."
"아! 그렇군요. 하지만 아시겠지만, 그건 우리 집 거위가 아닙니다."

"Indeed! Whose, / then?"
"정말인가요! 누구 거위죠, 그럼?"

"Well, / I got the two dozen / from a salesman / in
"음, 24마리를 샀지요 장사꾼에게

Covent Garden."
코벤트 가든의."

"Indeed? I know some of them. Which was it?"
"그런가요? 그쪽은 저도 좀 아는데. 어느 곳이었죠?"

"Breckinridge is his name."
"브레킨리지라는 이름이었죠."

"Ah! I don't know him. Well, / here's your good health
"아! 그 사람은 모르겠는데. 그럼, 건강을 빕니다,

landlord, / and prosperity to your house. Good-night."
그리고 사업도 번창하시길. 안녕히 계세요."

"Now for Mr. Breckinridge," / he continued, / buttoning
"이제 브레킨리지 씨에게 가지." 그가 말을 이었다, 코트 단추를

up his coat / as we came out / into the frosty air.
채우며 밖으로 나와 찬 공기를 쐬자.

here's 건배할 때 쓰는 말 | servitude 징역 | bitter end 막다른 최후, 막판 | slums 빈민가 | stall (시장의) 가판대, 좌판 | proprietor 소유주

"Remember, Watson / that though we have so homely
"기억하게, 왓슨　　　　　　　하찮은 것이 있을 뿐이지만

a thing / as a goose / at one end of this chain, / we have
거위같은　　　　이 일련의 사건 한쪽 끝에는,

at the other / a man who will certainly get seven years'
다른 쪽 끝에는 있네　7년의 징역형을 받게 될 것이 분명한 사람이

penal servitude / unless we can establish his innocence.
　　　　　　　우리가 그의 무죄를 입증하지 않으면.

It is possible / that our inquiry may but confirm his guilt;
가능성도 있어　　　우리 조사가 그의 유죄를 확인하는 것으로 그치게 될;

/ but, / in any case, / we have a line of investigation
하지만,　어느 경우든,　　　우리는 수사의 단서를 갖게 되었고

/ which has been missed by the police, / and which a
경찰이 놓쳐 버린,

singular chance has placed in our hands. Let us follow
특별한 기회가 우리 손 안에 있는 거야.　　　　　　　추적해 보자고

it / out to the bitter end. Faces to the south, / then, / and
　최후까지.　　　　　남쪽을 향해,　　　　그럼,

quick march!"
빨리 전진하세!"

We passed across Holborn, / down Endell Street, / and
우리는 홀본을 가로질러　　　　　엔델 가로 내려가서,

so through a zigzag of slums / to Covent Garden Market.
지그재그로 나 있는 빈민가를 통과해　　　코벤트 가든 시장에 도착했다.

One of the largest stalls / bore the name of Breckinridge
가장 큰 상점 중 한 곳에　　　　브레킨리지라는 간판이 붙어 있었는데,

upon it, / and the proprietor a horsey-looking man, / with
　　　　상점 주인은 얼굴이 말상인 남자로,

a sharp face and trim side-whiskers / was helping a boy
날카로운 얼굴에 깔끔하게 정돈된 구레나룻을 기른

to put up the shutters.
가게 문을 닫는 소년을 도와주고 있었다.

"Good-evening. It's a cold night," / said Holmes.
"안녕하십니까.   추운 밤이군요,"   홈즈가 말했다.

The salesman nodded / and shot a questioning glance / at
상인은 고개를 까딱하더니   미심쩍어 하는 눈초리로 쳐다보았다

my companion.
내 친구를.

"Sold out of geese, / I see," / continued Holmes, /
"거위는 다 팔렸군요,   보아하니,"   홈즈가 말을 이었다,

pointing at the bare slabs of marble.
비어 있는 대리석 좌판을 가리키며.

"Let you have five hundred / to-morrow morning."
"500마리 준비하겠소   내일 아침에."

"That's no good."
"그건 소용없어요."

"Well, / there are some / on the stall / with the gas-flare."
"그럼,   몇 마리 있을 거요   저 가게에   가스등이 켜져 있는."

"Ah, / but I was recommended to you."
"아,   하지만 여기를 추천 받았는데."

"Who by?"
"누구한테 말이오?"

"The landlord of the Alpha."
"알파인 주인장이오."

"Oh, yes; / I sent him a couple of dozen."
"아 그렇군;   그곳에 20여 마리 보냈지."

"Fine birds they were, / too. Now / where did you get
"좋은 거위더군요,   또한.   그런데   그 거위들은 어디에서 구했나요?"

them from?"

To my surprise / the question provoked a burst of anger /
놀랍게도   그 질문이 분노를 일으켰다

from the salesman.
상인에게.

"Now, / then, / mister," / said he, / with his head cocked
"이봐요,　　그럼,　　선생,"　　그가 말했다,　고개를 치켜들고

/ and his arms akimbo, / "what are you driving at? Let's
손을 허리에 댄 채,　　　　"의도가 뭡니까?

have it straight, / now."
솔직하게 말해 보시오,　이제."

"It is straight enough. I should like to know / who sold
"솔직하게 말했는데요.　　　알고 싶은 거요　　누가 당신에게

you the geese / which you supplied to the Alpha."
거위를 팔았는지　　알파인 선술집에 공급한."

"Well then, / I shan't tell you. So now!"
"그렇다면,　말하지 않겠소.　　이제 가시오!"

"Oh, / it is a matter of no importance; / but I don't know
"아,　그리 중요한 문제도 아닌데;　　　　모르겠군요

/ why you should be so warm / over such a trifle."
왜 그렇게 흥분하는 건지　　　　그런 사소한 일에."

"Warm! You'd be as warm, / maybe, / if you were as
"흥분이라고! 당신도 흥분했을 거요,　아마도,　나처럼 괴롭힘을 당하면.

pestered as I am. When I pay good money / for a good
나는 후한 값을 치르고　　　좋은 물건을 샀으니

article / there should be an end of the business; / but it's
그걸로 거래는 그만이지;　　　　　그런데

/ 'Where are the geese?' / and 'Who did you sell the
'거위는 어디 있소?' 라든가　　'누구에게 팔았소?'

geese to?' / and 'What will you take for the geese?' / One
또　'그 거위를 얼마에 팔겠소?' 라니

would think they were the only geese / in the world, / to
사람들이 거위가 그것뿐인 줄 알겠소　　이 세상에,

hear the fuss / that is made over them."
이런 야단 법석을 보면　그 거위 때문에 벌어진."

---

questioning 왜 그러느냐는 듯한, 미심쩍어 하는 | slab 평판, 판 | provoke 유발하다 | cock 위로 젖히다,
곧추세우다 | akimbo 손을 허리에 대고 | drive at ~을 의도하다 | pester 성가시게 하다, 괴롭히다

"Well, / I have no connection / with any other people
글쎄, 난 아무 관계가 없는데요 다른 사람들과는

/ who have been making inquiries," / said Holmes
그런 조사를 해 온," 홈즈가 무심하게 말했다.

carelessly.

"If you won't tell us / the bet is off, / that is all. But I'm
"당신이 말하지 않는다면 내기는 무효고, 그걸로 끝이오. 하지만 난

always ready to back my opinion / on a matter of fowls,
언제든지 기꺼이 내 생각에 돈을 걸 용의가 있소 거위에 대한 문제라면,

/ and I have a fiver on it / that the bird I ate / is country
5파운드를 걸지 내가 먹은 그 거위가 시골에서 키운

bred."
거라는 것에."

"Well, then, / you've lost your fiver, / for it's town bred,"
"흠, 그렇다면, 당신은 5파운드 잃은 거요, 그건 도시에서 키운 거니까,"

/ snapped the salesman.
상인이 쏘아붙였다.

"It's nothing of the kind."
"그건 그런 종류가 아니오."

"I say it is."
"그렇다니까."

"I don't believe it."
"믿을 수 없는데."

"D'you think / you know more about fowls / than I, /
"생각하는 거요 당신이 거위에 대해 더 많이 안다고 나보다,

who have handled them / ever since I was a nipper? I tell
거위를 다뤄온 어릴 때부터? 말하지만,

you, / all those birds / that went to the Alpha / were town
거위는 전부 알파인으로 보낸 도시에서 키운

bred."
거요."

---

back (내기에서) 돈을 걸다 | fiver 5파운드(짜리 지폐) | snap 화난 목소리로 딱딱거리다, 톡 쏘다 | nipper 어린
아이 | sovereign 1파운드짜리 금화(영국의 구 화폐) | obstinate 고집 센, 완강한 | grimly 냉혹하게, 무섭게

"You'll never persuade me / to believe that."
"절대 날 설득할 수 없을 거요   그 얘기를 믿도록."

"Will you bet, / then?"
"내기하겠소,   그럼?"

"It's merely taking your money, / for I know / that I am
"당신 돈만 잃을 텐데,   난 알고 있으니까   내가 옳다는 걸.

right. But I'll have a sovereign on with you, / just to
하지만 금화 1파운드를 걸겠소,   당신에게 가르치기

teach you / not to be obstinate."
위해서   고집 부리지 말라고."

The salesman chuckled grimly.
상인은 냉혹하게 웃었다.

"Bring me the books, / Bill," / said he.
"장부를 갖고 와,   빌."   그가 말했다.

The small boy brought round / a small thin volume / and
소년이 갖고 와서   얇은 장부 한 권과

a great greasy-backed one, / laying them out together /
기름때가 덕지덕지 묻은 큰 장부 한 권을,   함께 올려 놓았다

beneath the hanging lamp.
매달린 전등 밑에.

"Now then, / Mr. Cocksure," / said the salesman, / "I
"자 이제, 자신만만한 양반." 상인이 말했다,

thought / that I was out of geese, / but before I finish /
"생각했는데 거위를 다 팔았다고, 하지만 끝내기 전에

you'll find / that there is still one left / in my shop. You
보게 되겠군 아직 한 마리 값이 남은 걸 내 가게에서.

see this little book?"
이 장부가 보이시오?"

"Well?"
"그런데요?"

"That's the list of the folk / from whom I buy. D'you
"이런 사람들의 명단이오 내가 거위를 산. 알겠소?

see? Well, / then, / here on this page are the country folk,
자, 그럼, 여기 이 페이지에 있는 게 시골 사람들의 명단이고,

/ and the numbers after their names are / where their
이름 뒤에 쓰여 있는 숫자는 그들과의 거래 내역이

accounts are / in the big ledger. Now, then! You see this
적힌 곳이오 큰 장부에서. 자, 그럼! 빨간 잉크로 쓰여 있는

other page in red ink? Well, / that is a list of my town
다른 페이지가 보이죠? 자, 그건 도시 거래처의 명단이오.

suppliers. Now, / look at that third name. Just read it out
자, 세 번째 이름을 보시오. 큰 소리로 읽어 보시지."

to me."

"Mrs. Oakshott, / 117, Brixton Road — 249," / read
"오크쇼트 부인, 브릭스턴 가 117번지 — 249페이지,"

Holmes.
홈즈가 읽었다.

"Quite so. Now turn that up / in the ledger."
"그렇소. 이제 그곳을 찾아보지 큰 장부에서."

Holmes turned to the page indicated.
홈즈는 그 페이지를 넘겼다.

cocksure 자신만만한 | ledger 거래 장부

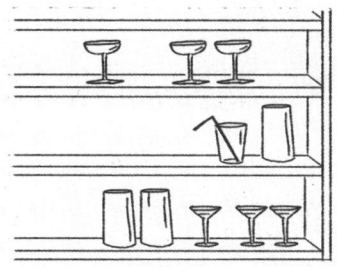

"Here you are, / 'Mrs. Oakshott, / 117, Brixton Road, /
"여기 있군, '오크쇼트 부인, 브릭스턴 가 117번지,

egg and poultry supplier.' "
달걀과 가금류 공급자.' "

"Now, / then, / what's the last entry?"
"이제, 그럼, 마지막에는 뭐라고 적혀 있소?"

"'December 22nd. Twenty-four geese at 7s. 6d.'"
" '12월 22일. 거위 24마리에 7실링 6펜스.' "

"Quite so. There you are. And underneath?"
"그렇소. 바로 그거요. 그럼 그 밑에는?"

"'Sold to Mr. Windigate of the Alpha, / at 12s.' "
" '알파인의 윈드게이트에게 판매, 12실링에.' "

"What have you to say now?"
"자 이제 뭐라고 말 좀 해 보시지?"

Sherlock Holmes looked deeply chagrined. He drew a
셜록 홈즈는 매우 분한 듯 보였다. 그는 금화를 꺼내

sovereign / from his pocket / and threw it down upon
주머니에서 가판대에 던지고는,

the slab, / turning away / with the air of a man / whose
돌아서 나갔다 태도를 보이며

disgust is too deep for words. A few yards off / he
화가 나서 말이 안 나오는 듯한. 좀 떨어진 곳에서

stopped under a lamp-post / and laughed in the hearty, /
그는 가로등 아래 멈추더니 마음껏 웃었다,

noiseless fashion / which was peculiar to him.
소리 없이 그의 주특기인.

"When you see a man / with whiskers of that cut / and
"사람을 보면 구레나룻을 저렇게 자르고

the '*Pink'un' protruding out of his pocket, / you can
주머니 밖으로 '핑컨' 이 빠져 나와 있는,

always draw him by a bet," / said he.
언제나 내기를 걸 수 있지," 그가 말했다.

---

* 1865년에 창간되어 1932년에 폐간된 영국의 주간 스포츠 잡지 '더 스포팅 타임즈' (The Sport-ing Times)를 일컫는 이름. 분홍색 종이에 인쇄되었다고 해서 '핑컨' (Pink' un)이라 불렸다.

"I daresay that / if I had put £100 down / in front of him,
"아마도 내가 100파운드를 내놓았더라도 그의 앞에,

/ that man would not have given me / such complete
그 남자는 알려 주지 않았을 거야 그런 확실한 정보를

information / as was drawn from him / by the idea / that
그에게서 이끌어 낸 생각으로

he was doing me on a wager. Well, Watson, / we are, / I
자신이 내게 내기를 하고 있다는. 자, 왓슨, 우린,

fancy, / nearing the end of our quest, / and the only point
내 생각에, 조사의 막바지에 도달한 것 같군, 그러니 유일한 점은

/ which remains to be determined is / whether we should
결정해야 할 바로 가야 할지의 문제라네

go on / to this Mrs. Oakshott / to-night, / or whether
오크쇼트 부인에게, 오늘 밤에,

we should reserve it for to-morrow. It is clear / from
혹은 찾아가는 걸 내일로 미뤄야 할지. 분명해

what that surly fellow said / that there are others besides
저 퉁명스런 남자가 말한 것으로 볼 때 우리 외에 다른 사람들이 있는 것이

ourselves / who are anxious about the matter, / and I
그 일에 대해 알고 싶어 하는 사람들이,

should — "
그러니 나는 — "

Key Expression 🎯

here you are의 의미

here you are은 '여기 있네'라는 의미로, 물건을 건네줄 때, 목적지에 도착했을 때, 찾던 것을 찾았을 때 주로 사용하는 표현입니다.
here it is로 바꾸어 쓰기도 합니다.

ex) Here you are.
여기 있군.

poultry 가금(닭, 오리, 거위 따위) | chagrined 분하게 여기는 | daresay 아마도 ~일 것이다(=dare say) | wager
내기, 도박 | surly 퉁명스런

A. 다음 문장을 해석해 보세요.

(1) I observe / that your circulation is / more adapted for summer / than for winter.
→

(2) He spoke / in a slow staccato fashion, / choosing his words with care, / and gave the impression generally / of a man of learning and letters / who had had ill-usage / at the hands of fortune.
→

(3) Though we have so homely a thing / as a goose / at one end of this chain, / we have at the other / a man who will certainly get seven years' penal servitude / unless we can establish his innocence.
→

(4) I daresay that / if I had put £100 down / in front of him, / that man would not have given me / such complete information / as was drawn from him / by the idea / that he was doing me on a wager.
→

B. 다음 주어진 문구가 알맞은 문장이 되도록 순서를 맞춰 보세요.

(1) 예전처럼 제게 돈이 넉넉하게 있는 게 아니라서요.
(been / so / Shillings / not / me / plentiful / have / with)

_____ as they once were.

(2) 그렇게 하지 않았다면 상해 버려 아무 쓸모가 없었을 겁니다.
(so / we / done / not / had)
It would have been of no use to anyone _____.

A. (1) 제가 보기에 베이커 씨는 겨울보다 여름에 더 잘 적응하실 것 같네요. (2) 그는 느리고 끊어지는 스타카토 같은 말투로 조심스럽게 단어를 선택하여 말해서, 전체적으로 학식과 교양을 갖췄지만 경제적 형편 때문에 이를 제대로 사용하지 못했던 사람이라는 인상을 풍겼다. (3) 이 일련의 사건의 한쪽 끝에는 거위 같은 하찮은 것이 있을 뿐이지만, 다른 쪽 끝에는 우리가 그의 무죄를 입증하지 않으면 7년의 징역형을 받

140 The Adventure of the Blue Carbuncle

(3) 당신네 맥주가 거위만큼만 좋다면 맛이 뛰어나겠군요.
(geese / good / is / if / as / your / it / as)
Your beer should be excellent _____ .

(4) 그건 전혀 중요한 문제가 아닙니다.
(importance / matter / no / a / is / of / it)
→

C. 다음 주어진 문장이 본문의 내용과 맞으면 T, 틀리면 F에 동그라미 하세요.

(1) Henry Baker knew nothing about the Blue Carbuncle.
(T / F)

(2) Henry Baker seemed to be in a bad condition economically.
(T / F)

(3) Sherlock Holmes got information about the goose' breeder
from the owner of Alpha Inn.
(T / F)

(4) There must be another person who wanted to know about the
toose.
(T / F)

D. 의미가 비슷한 것끼리 서로 연결해 보세요.

(1) geniality   ▶   ◀ ① assume

(2) presume   ▶   ◀ ② confident

(3) institute   ▶   ◀ ③ launch

(4) cocksure   ▶   ◀ ④ kindness

His remarks were suddenly cut short / by a loud hubbub
홈즈의 말이 갑자기 끊겼다   고함 소리 때문에

/ which broke out from the stall / which we had just left.
가게에서 터져 나온   방금 전에 들렀던.

Turning round / we saw a little rat-faced fellow standing
돌아보니   얼굴이 쥐처럼 생긴 남자가 서 있는 것이 보였다

/ in the centre of the circle of yellow light / which was
노란 불빛 가운데에

thrown by the swinging lamp, / while Breckinridge, / the
흔들리는 등이 비추는,   한편 브레킨리지는,

salesman, / framed in the door of his stall, / was shaking
상인인,   상점 문 앞에 서 있던,   사납게 주먹을 휘두

his fists fiercely / at the cringing figure.
르고 있었다   움츠리고 있는 사람에게.

"I've had enough of you and your geese," / he shouted.
"네놈이나 네놈 거위 얘긴 더 이상 못 참겠어,"   그가 소리쳤다.

"I wish you were all at the devil together. If you come
"당신들 모두 지옥으로 꺼져 버렸으면 좋겠군.

pestering me any more / with your silly talk / I'll set
다시 와서 나를 괴롭히면   그런 멍청한 얘기로

the dog at you. You bring Mrs. Oakshott here / and I'll
개를 풀어놓을 테다.   오크쇼트 부인을 이리 데려와

answer her, / but what have you to do with it? Did I buy
그럼 대답해 주지,   하지만 그게 네놈이랑 무슨 상관이 있지?   내가 그 거위로

the geese off you?"
사기라도 쳤단 말이냐?"

"No; / but one of them was mine / all the same," /
"아니요, 하지만 그 거위 중 한 마리는 제 것이었어요 어쨌든,"

whined the little man.
사내가 울먹였다.

"Well, then, / ask Mrs. Oakshott for it."
그럼, 오크쇼트 부인에게 물어보든지."

"She told me to ask you."
"부인은 당신에게 물어보라 하던데요."

"Well, / you can ask the King of Proosia, / for all I care.
"흥, 그럼 프러시아 왕에게 가서 물어보든지, 난 상관 없으니.

I've had enough of it. Get out of this!"
이제 진절머리가 나. 썩 꺼져!"

He rushed fiercely forward, / and the inquirer flitted
그가 난폭하게 쫓아오자, 질문하던 사람은 황급히 달아나 버렸다

away / into the darkness.
어둠 속으로.

"Ha! This may save us a visit to Brixton Road," /
"허! 이걸로 브릭스턴까지 가지 않아도 되겠는걸,"

whispered Holmes.
홈즈가 속삭였다.

"Come with me, / and we will see / what is to be made of
"같이 가지, 알아 보세 저 사내에게 무슨 일이 있었는지."

this fellow."

Striding through the scattered knots of people / who
흩어져 있는 사람들 무리를 뚫고 걸어가

lounged round the flaring stalls, / my companion
불이 환하게 밝혀진 가게 주위에서 서성이던.

speedily overtook the little man / and touched him upon
홈즈는 그 남자를 빠르게 따라잡더니 어깨를 쳤다.

the shoulder. He sprang round, / and I could see / in the
그가 깜짝 놀라며 돌아보자, 보였다 가스등 불빛

gas-light / that every vestige of colour had been driven
아래에서 붉으락푸르락해진 그의 얼굴이.

from his face.

---

hubbub 왁자지껄한 소리 | cringing 움츠린 | have had enough of ~으로 족하다, 질색이다, 더 이상 못 참다 |
pester 조르다, 보채다 | buy off 뇌물로 매수하다 | all the same 어쨌든 | whine 징징거리다, 우는 소리를 하다 |
for all I care 신경쓰지 않는다 | flit 휙 지나가다 | scattered 흩어져 있는 | vestige 증거, 흔적

143

"Who are you, / then? What do you want?" / he asked /
"누구요,　　　　그런데? 원하는 게 뭡니까?"　　　　그가 물었다

in a quavering voice.
떨리는 목소리로.

"You will excuse me," / said Holmes blandly, / "but I
"실례지만,"　　　　　홈즈가 부드럽게 말했다.

could not help overhearing the questions / which you
"우연히 듣고 말았습니다

put to the salesman / just now. I think / that I could be of
당신이 저 상인에게 하는 말을　　방금 전에.　　내 생각에

assistance to you."
도움이 될 수 있을 것 같은데."

"You? Who are you? How could you know anything of
"당신이? 당신 누구요?　　　당신이 그 일에 대해 어떻게 아시죠?"

the matter?"

"My name is Sherlock Holmes. It is my business / to
"내 이름은 셜록 홈즈요.　　　　　내 일이죠　　　알아

know / what other people don't know."
내는 게　　다른 사람들이 모르는 일을."

Key Expression

can't help -ing : ~하지 않을 수 없다

조동사 can과 동명사를 이용한 숙어 표현으로 '~하지 않을 수 없다', 즉 '~할 수
밖에 없다'라는 뜻입니다.
같은 의미의 다음 숙어들을 함께 외워두세요. 특히 to 부정사와 동명사의 쓰임
에 유의하세요.

▶ cannot help -ing
= caannot but + 동사원형
= cannot choose but + 동사원형
= have no choice but to + 동사원형

ex) I could not help overhearing the questions which you put to the salesman just
now.
당신이 방금 전에 저 상인에게 한 질문을 우연히 듣고 말았습니다.

"But you can know nothing of this?"
하지만 이 일은 모를 텐데요?"

"Excuse me, / I know everything of it. You are
"미안하지만,   난 모든 걸 알고 있소.

endeavouring to trace some geese / which were sold by
당신은 어떤 거위를 추적하느라 애쓰고 있지요   오크쇼트 부인이 팔았고,

Mrs. Oakshott, / of Brixton Road, / to a salesman named
브릭스턴 가의,   브레킨리지라는 이름의 상인에게,

Breckinridge, / by him / in turn to Mr. Windigate, / of
그리고 그는   윈디게이트 씨에게 팔았고,

the Alpha, / and by him to his club, / of which Mr. Henry
알파인의,   그는 자신의 클럽에 넘겼죠,

Baker is a member."
헨리 베이커라는 회원에게."

"Oh, sir, / you are the very man / whom I have longed to
"오, 선생님,   바로 그분이시군요   제가 찾아 헤매던,

meet," / cried the little fellow / with outstretched hands /
남자가 소리쳤다   두 팔을 내밀고

and quivering fingers.
손을 부들부들 떨며.

"I can hardly explain to you / how interested I am / in
"말로 할 수 없을 정도죠   제가 얼마나 관심을 갖고 있는지

this matter."
이 문제에."

Sherlock Holmes hailed a four-wheeler / which was
셜록 홈즈는 사륜 마차를 불러 세웠다   지나가던.

passing.

"In that case / we had better discuss it / in a cosy room /
"그런 경우에는   얘기하는 게 낫죠   아늑한 방에서

rather than in this wind-swept market-place," / said he.
이렇게 바람이 쌩쌩 부는 시장보다는,"   그가 말했다.

---

quavering 떨리는 | blandly 담백하게, 부드럽게 | long to ~하고 싶은 생각이 간절하다 | outstretched 죽 뻗은
| hail 불러 세우다

"But pray tell me, / before we go farther, / who it is that /
그런데 말씀해 주시죠,   출발하기 전에,   도대체 누구신지

I have the pleasure of assisting."
제가 도와드릴 분이."

The man hesitated / for an instant.
남자는 머뭇거렸다   잠시 동안.

"My name is John Robinson," / he answered / with a
"제 이름은 존 로빈슨입니다."   그가 대답했다

sidelong glance.
곁눈질을 하며.

"No, no; / the real name," / said Holmes sweetly.
"아니, 아니; 진짜 이름이요,"   홈즈가 상냥하게 말했다.

"It is always awkward / doing business with an alias."
"늘 곤란하거든요   가명을 쓰는 사람과 일하는 것은."

A flush sprang to the white cheeks of the stranger.
낯선 남자의 흰 뺨이 순간 붉게 물들었다.

"Well then," / said he, / "my real name is James Ryder."
"그렇다면,"   그가 말했다,   "제 본명은 제임스 라이더입니다."

"Precisely so. Head attendant at the Hotel Cosmopolitan.
"그렇군.   코스모폴리탄 호텔의 지배인이군요.

Pray step into the cab, / and I shall soon be able to tell
마차에 오르시오,   그러면 곧 말씀 드리겠소

you / everything which you would wish to know."
    당신이 알고 싶어 하는 걸 전부."

sidelong 곁눈질의 | awkward 곤란한, 어색한 | alias ～이라는 가명으로 알려진 | windfall 뜻밖의 횡재 |
catastrophe 재앙

The little man stood / glancing from one to the other of
그 남자는 서서 / 우리를 번갈아 쳐다보았다

us / with half-frightened, half-hopeful eyes, / as one who
놀람과 희망이 반씩 섞인 눈빛으로, / 확신하지 못하는

is not sure / whether he is on the verge of a windfall / or
사람처럼 / 자신이 뜻밖의 횡재를 만난 것인지

of a catastrophe. Then / he stepped into the cab, / and in
재앙을 만난 것인지. / 그리고는 / 마차에 올랐고,

half an hour / we were back / in the sitting-room at Baker
30분이 채 안 되어 / 우리는 돌아왔다 / 베이커 가 하숙집의 거실로.

Street. Nothing had been said / during our drive, / but
아무 말도 없었다 / 마차를 타고 오는 동안,

the high, thin breathing of our new companion, / and the
하지만 새로운 동료의 높고 가는 숨소리와,

claspings and unclaspings of his hands, / spoke of the
두 손을 쥐었다 폈다 하는 모습으로 보아,

nervous tension within him.
심하게 긴장한 듯 보였다.

"Here we are!" / said Holmes cheerily / as we filed into
"다 왔소!" / 홈즈가 명랑하게 말했다 / 방 안으로 들어서며.

the room.

"The fire looks very seasonable / in this weather. You
"난로가 제격이지 / 이런 날씨에는.

look cold, / Mr. Ryder. Pray take the basket-chair. I will
추워 보이는군요. / 라이더 씨. / 버들가지 의자에 앉으시오.

just put on my slippers / before we settle this little matter
난 실내화로 갈아 신어야겠소 / 당신의 문제를 해결하기 전에.

of yours. Now, then! You want to know / what became of
자, 그럼! / 당신은 알고 싶은 거죠 / 그 거위들이 어떻게 되었

those geese?"
는지?"

"Yes, sir."
"그렇습니다."

"Or rather, / I fancy, / of that goose. It was one bird, / I
"더 정확히 하자면 내 생각에,   그 거위라고 해야겠군. 한 마리였을 테니,

imagine / in which you were interested / — white, / with
내 생각에   당신이 관심 있는 놈은   — 흰색의,

a black bar across the tail."
꼬리에 검은 줄이 있는 거위지."

Ryder quivered / with emotion.
라이더는 몸을 떨었다   흥분해서.

"Oh, sir," / he cried, / "can you tell me / where it went
"오, 선생님,"   그가 소리쳤다,   "알려 주실 수 있습니까   그 거위가 어디로 갔는

to?"
지?"

"It came here."
"여기로 왔소."

"Here?"
"여기라고요? "

Key Expression ❢

감탄문 만들기

영어의 감탄문은 what과 how로 시작하는 두 가지가 있어요.
what은 명사가 있는 문장에, how는 형용사나 부사의 문장에 사용하는데 각각
의 어순을 잘 기억해 두세요.

▶ What + (a / an) + 형용사 + 명사 + (주어 + 동사)!
▶ How + 형용사 / 부사 + (주어 + 동사)!

ex) What a shrimp it is, to be sure!
정말 약해빠진 친구로군!
How beautiful you are!
당신은 정말 아름답군요!

stagger 비틀거리다 | mantelpiece 벽난로 위 선반, 맨틀피스 | strong-box 금고 | drawn face 찡그린 얼굴 |
felony 중죄, 흉악 범죄 | impunity 처벌을 받지 않음

"Yes, / and a most remarkable bird / it proved. I don't
"그렇소, 그런데 아주 별난 거위더군 알고 보니. 놀라운 일이

wonder / that you should take an interest in it. It laid
아니지 당신이 그 거위에 관심을 갖는 것도. 알을 하나

an egg / after it was dead / — the bonniest, brightest
낳았는데 죽고 난 후 — 가장 예쁘고, 빛나는 작은 파란 알이었소

little blue egg / that ever was seen. I have it here / in my
내가 본 것 중. 이곳에 보관하고 있소

museum."
내 박물관에."

Our visitor staggered to his feet / and clutched the
손님은 비틀거리며 일어서서 벽난로 선반을 붙잡았다

mantelpiece / with his right hand. Holmes unlocked his
오른손으로. 홈즈는 금고를 열고

strong-box / and held up the blue carbuncle, / which
푸른 카벙클을 꺼냈다,

shone out like a star, / with a cold, brilliant, / many-
보석은 별처럼 빛났다, 차갑게 반짝이는,

pointed radiance. Ryder stood glaring / with a drawn
영롱한 광채를 뿜어내며. 라이더는 바라보며 서 있었다 찡그린 얼굴로,

face, / uncertain / whether to claim / or to disown it.
모르겠다는 듯이 소유권을 주장해야 할지 말아야 할지.

"The game's up, / Ryder," / said Holmes quietly.
"게임은 끝났네, 라이더," 홈즈가 조용히 말했다.

"Hold up, man, / or you'll be into the fire! Give him an
"똑바로 서게, 그렇지 않으면 난로 속으로 넘어지겠네! 저 친구 좀 부축해서

arm back / into his chair, / Watson. He's not got blood /
의자에 앉혀 주게, 왓슨. 그런 사람도 아니었군

enough to go in for felony / with impunity. Give him a
중죄에 가담할 만한 태연하게. 저 자에게 브랜디

dash of brandy. So! Now / he looks a little more human.
한 잔 주게. 그래! 이제야 좀 사람처럼 보이는군.

What a shrimp it is, / to be sure!"
약해빠진 친구로군, 정말!"

For a moment / he had staggered and nearly fallen, / but
잠시 동안　　　　　그는 비틀거리며 거의 쓰러질 듯 했지만,

the brandy brought / a tinge of colour into his cheeks, /
브랜디가 들어가자　　　뺨에 화색이 돌더니,

and he sat staring / with frightened eyes / at his accuser.
자리에 앉아 쳐다보았다　　놀란 눈으로　　　　자신을 비난하는 사람을.

"I have almost every link in my hands, / and all the
"사건의 거의 모든 연결 고리는 내 손 안에 있네,　　　그리고 모든 증거도

proofs / which I could possibly need, / so there is little /
확보했지　　내가 필요로 하는,　　　　　　별로 없지

which you need tell me. Still, / that little may as well be
자네한테 들어야 할 얘기도.　　그래도,　　확실히 해 두는 게 좋겠지

cleared up / to make the case complete. You had heard, /
　　　　사건을 마무리 지으려면.　　　　　사전에 들었지,

Ryder, / of this blue stone of the Countess of Morcar's?"
라이더,　　모르카 백작 부인의 이 푸른 카벙클에 대해서?"

"It was Catherine Cusack / who told me of it," / said he /
"캐서린 쿠삭이었습니다　　그것에 대해 얘기해 준 사람은,"　그가 말했다

in a crackling voice.
갈라지는 목소리로.

Key Expression ♥

may as well : ~하는 것이 낫다

may as well 은 '~하는 것이 낫다'로 had better와 같은 의미로 쓰입니다.
조동사 may의 영향으로 뒤에는 동사 원형이 옵니다.
비슷한 형태의 may well은 '~하는 것이 당연하다'라는 의미이니 혼동하지 않
도록 주의하세요.

ex) Still, that little may as well be cleared up to make the case complete.
그래도, 사건을 마무리 지으려면. 그 점을 확실히 해 두는 게 좋겠지.

sudden wealth 돈벼락, 벼락부자 | scrupulous 양심적인 | villain 악당 | confederate 공범 | shriek 소리를
지르다

"I see / — her ladyship's waiting-maid. Well, / the
"그렇군 — 부인의 하녀 말이군. 그래,

temptation of sudden wealth / so easily acquired / was
돈벼락의 유혹을 그렇게 손쉽게 얻을 수 있는

too much for you, / as it has been for better men / before
자제하기 힘들었겠지, 더 부자인 사람들도 그랬으니 자네 이전

you; / but you were not very scrupulous / in the means
에; 하지만 자네는 비양심적이었네 사용한 수법이.

you used. It seems to me, / Ryder, / that there is the
내가 보기에, 라이더,

making of a very pretty villain / in you. You knew / that
매우 악한 기질이 있는 것 같군 자네 안에는. 자네는 알고 있었어

this man Horner, / the plumber, / had been concerned / in
호너라는 남자가, 배관공인, 관련된 적이 있었다는 것을

some such matter / before, / and that suspicion would rest
그런 문제에 전에도, 그래서 의심이 쏠릴 것이라고

/ the more readily / upon him. What did you do, / then?
더 쉽게 그에게. 어떻게 했느냐고, 그 다음엔?

You made some small job / in my lady's room / — you
일을 꾸며 놓고 백작 부인의 방에

and your confederate Cusack — / and you managed /
— 공범인 쿠삭과 함께 — 처리했지

that he should be the man sent for. Then, / when he had
호너가 불려 오도록. 그리고, 그가 떠나자,

left, / you rifled the jewel-case, / raised the alarm, / and
보석함을 뒤지고, 경보를 울려서,

had this unfortunate man arrested. You then —"
이 불운한 남자가 체포된 것이지. 그 다음엔--"

Ryder threw himself down suddenly upon the rug / and
라이더는 갑자기 바닥에 몸을 내던지며

clutched at my companion's knees.
내 친구의 무릎을 움켜잡았다.

"For God's sake, / have mercy!" / he shrieked.
"제발, 봐 주십시오!" 그가 소리쳤다.

"Think of my father! Of my mother! It would break their
"제 아버지를 생각해 주세요!   제 어머니를요!   그분들의 마음이 찢어지실 거예요.

hearts. I never went wrong before! I never will again. I
전 나쁜 짓을 한 적이 없었어요!   다시는 그러지 않을 겁니다.

swear it. I'll swear it on a Bible. Oh, / don't bring it into
맹세합니다.   성경에 대고 맹세합니다.   오,   제발 법정에 넘기지 말아 주세요!

court! For Christ's sake, / don't!"
제발,   그러지 마세요!"

"Get back into your chair!" / said Holmes sternly.
"다시 의자에 앉게!"   홈즈가 단호하게 말했다.

"It is very well to cringe and crawl now, / but you
"지금 엎드려 기는 것도 좋겠지만,

thought little enough / of this poor Horner / in the dock
생각은 조금도 하지 않았군   불쌍한 호너에 대해서

for a crime of / which he knew nothing."
죄를 뒤집어 쓰고 있는   아무것도 모른 채."

"I will fly, / Mr. Holmes. I will leave the country, / sir.
'도망치겠습니다, 홈즈 씨.   이 나라를 떠나겠어요.   선생님.

Then / the charge against him / will break down."
그러면   그에 대한 혐의는   벗겨질 거예요."

"Hum! We will talk about that. And now let us hear / a
"흠!   그 얘기는 나중에 하지.   그럼 이제 들어보지

true account of the next act. How came the stone into the
그 다음 행동에 대한 설명을.   어떻게 그 보석이 거위 뱃속으로 들어갔는지,

goose, / and how came the goose into the open market?
그리고 거위가 어떻게 시장에 나오게 되었는지?

Tell us the truth, / for there lies your only hope of safety."
사실을 말하게,   자네가 안전할 수 있는 길은 그것 뿐이니까."

Ryder passed his tongue / over his parched lips.
라이더는 혀를 움직여   바싹 마른 입술을 축였다.

"I will tell you it / just as it happened, / sir," / said he.
"말씀 드리겠습니다   일어난 그대로,   선생님," 그가 말했다.

---

sternly 엄격하게 | cringe 움츠리다 | crawl 기다 | dock (법정의) 피고석 | parched 몹시 건조한 | take it into
one's head 갑자기 생각하기 시작하다 | commission 위원회 | fatten 살지우다 | detective 수사관, 탐정

"When Horner had been arrested, / it seemed to me / that
"호너가 체포되었을 때, 제 생각에

it would be best for me to get away / with the stone / at
도망치는 게 가장 좋을 것 같았습니다 보석을 갖고

once, / for I did not know / at what moment the police
즉시, 몰랐으니까요 언제 경찰이 생각하게 될지

might not take it into their heads / to search me and
저와 제 방을 뒤지려고.

my room. There was no place about the hotel / where it
호텔에는 없었습니다

would be safe. I went out, / as if on some commission, /
안전한 장소가. 저는 밖으로 나가서, 무슨 할 일이 있는 것처럼,

and I made for my sister's house. She had married a man
누나 집으로 갔습니다. 누나는 오크쇼트란 남자와 결혼해서,

named Oakshott, / and lived in Brixton Road, / where
브릭스턴 가에 살고 있는데,

she fattened fowls for the market.
그곳에서 거위를 길러 시장에 내다 팔았지요.

All the way there / every man I met / seemed to me to
그곳까지 가는 동안 만나는 모든 사람들이

be a policeman or a detective; / and, / for all that it was
내게는 경찰이나 탐정처럼 보였습니다; 그래서, 추운 밤이었는데도,

a cold night, / the sweat was pouring down my face /
얼굴에 땀이 쏟아졌습니다

before I came to the Brixton Road. My sister asked me /
브릭스턴 가에 도착하기도 전에. 누나는 물었지만

what was the matter, / and why I was so pale; / but I told
무슨 일이 있었느냐고, 얼굴이 왜 그렇게 창백하냐고; 저는 말했지요

her / that I had been upset / by the jewel robbery / at the
당황한 것이라고 보석 절도 사건 때문에 호텔에서

hotel. Then / I went into the back yard / and smoked a
일어난. 그리고 뒷마당으로 가서 담배를 피우며

pipe / and wondered / what it would be best to do.
생각했습니다 어떻게 하는 게 가장 좋을지.

I had a friend once called Maudsley, / who went to the
제게는 모즐리라는 친구가 있습니다,   그는 나쁜 짓을 해서,

bad, / and has just been serving his time / in Pentonville.
막 형기를 마쳤지요   펜턴빌 감옥에서.

One day / he had met me, / and fell into talk / about the
어느 날   그 친구가 저를 만나,   이야기를 한 적이 있어요

ways of thieves, / and how they could get rid of / what
도둑들의 방법에 대해,   어떻게 처리하는지

they stole. I knew / that he would be true to me, / for I
훔친 물건을.   저는 알았죠   그의 얘기가 사실이라는 걸,

knew one or two things about him; / so I made up my
그에 대해 좀 알고 있으니까요;   그래서 결심했습니다

mind / to go right on to Kilburn, / where he lived, / and
마음   킬번으로 가서,   그가 살고 있는,

take him into my confidence. He would show me / how
비밀을 털어놓기로.   제게 알려 줄 테니까요

to turn the stone into money. But how to get to him / in
보석을 어떻게 돈으로 바꿀 수 있을지.   하지만 어떻게 그에게 갈 수 있을까요

safety? I thought of the agonies / I had gone through /
안전하게?   그 고통이 생각났어요   제가 겪은

in coming from the hotel. I might / at any moment / be
호텔에서 오는 동안.   어쩌면   어느 순간에

seized and searched, / and there would be the stone
잡혀서 수색 당할지도 모르니까요,   보석이 들어있는데

in my waistcoat pocket. I was leaning against the wall
제 조끼 주머니 속에.   벽에 기대어 서서

/ at the time / and looking at the geese / which were
   그때   거위들을 바라보고 있는데

waddling about / round my feet, / and suddenly / an idea
뒤뚱거리며 돌아다니는   제 발 밑에서,   갑자기

came into my head / which showed me / how I could beat
생각이 떠올랐습니다   알려 주는   속일 수 있는 방법을

/ the best detective that ever lived.
   어떤 유능한 탐정이라도.

agony 극도의 고통 | waddle 뒤뚱뒤뚱 걷다

My sister had told me / some weeks before that / I might
누나가 말한 적이 있습니다   몇 주 전에

have the pick of her geese / for a Christmas present, /
누나의 거위 중 한 마리를 고를 수 있다고   크리스마스 선물로,

and I knew / that she was always as good as her word. I
그리고 알고 있었죠   누나는 항상 약속을 지킨다는 것을.

would take my goose now, / and in it / I would carry my
그때 제 거위를 잡는다면,   그 안에 넣어서, 보석을 넣어 운반할 수 있겠

stone / to Kilburn. There was a little shed / in the yard, /
지요   킬번까지.   작은 헛간이 하나 있었는데   마당에는,

and behind this / I drove one of the birds / — a fine big
그 뒤로   거위 한 마리를 몰았습니다   — 살지고 좋은 놈으로.

one, / white, / with a barred tail. I caught it, / and prying
흰색에,   꼬리에 줄무늬가 있는.   저는 거위를 잡아,

its bill open, / I thrust the stone down its throat / as far as
부리를 열고,   보석을 목구멍으로 밀어 넣었습니다

my finger could reach. The bird gave a gulp, / and I felt
손가락이 닿는 한 깊숙이.   거위는 보석을 삼켰고,   느껴졌어요

/ the stone pass along its gullet / and down into its crop.
보석이 거위의 식도를 지나   모이주머니 안으로 내려가는 것이.

But the creature flapped and struggled, / and out came
하지만 거위가 퍼덕거리며 몸부림을 쳐서,   누나가 밖으로 나왔고

my sister / to know what was the matter. As I turned to
무슨 일이 벌어졌는지 알게 되었죠.   누나에게 설명하려고

speak to her / the brute broke loose / and fluttered off /
돌아서는 순간   그 놈은 빠져나가   파닥이며 달아나버렸습니다

among the others.
무리들 사이로.

'Whatever were you doing / with that bird, / Jem?' / says
'뭘 하고 있었던 거야   거위를 갖고,   젬?'

she.
누나가 물었어요.

shed 헛간 | barred 가로줄무늬가 있는 | pry 비틀어 열다 | thrust 밀다 | gulp 꿀꺽꿀꺽 삼키다 | gullet 식도 |
flap 퍼덕거리다 | brute 동물 | flutter 파닥이다, 훨훨 날아가다 | yonder 저기 보이는 | all the same 아무래도
좋은, 똑같은 | huff 화가 나서 씩씩거리다

'Well,' / said I, / 'you said you'd give me one / for
'음,' 제가 말했죠, '누나가 거위 한 마리를 준다고 했잖아

Christmas, / and I was feeling / which was the fattest.'
크리스마스 선물로, 그래서 만져보고 있었어 어떤 놈이 제일 통통한지.'

'Oh,' / says she, / 'we've set yours aside for you / —
'오,' 누나가 말했죠, '네 것은 따로 준비해놨어

Jem's bird, we call it. It's the big white one over yonder.
— 젬의 거위라고 부르지. 저기 보이는 크고 하얀 놈이야.

There's twenty-six of them, / which makes one for you, /
스물여섯 마리가 있는데, 하나는 네 것이고,

and one for us, / and two dozen for the market.'
하나는 우리 것, 나머지 스물 네 마리는 시장에 팔 거야'

'Thank you, / Maggie,' / says I; / 'but / if it is all the
'고마워, 매기 누나,' 내가 말했죠; '하지만 누나에게 아무래도 좋다면,

same to you, / I'd rather have that one / I was handling
난 저 거위를 갖고 싶어 방금 만져보고 있던.'

just now.'

'The other is a good three pound heavier,' / said she, /
'다른 놈이 3파운드나 더 나가는 데.' 누나가 말했죠,

'and we fattened it expressly for you.'
'그리고 널 위해 특별히 살지웠다고.'

'Never mind. I'll have the other, / and I'll take it now,' /
'괜찮아. 난 다른 놈으로 할래, 그리고 지금 가져갈게,'

said I.
제가 말했어요.

'Oh, / just as you like,' / said she, / a little huffed.
'아, 좋을대로 해,' 누나가 말했죠. 약간 화를 내며.

'Which is it you want, / then?'
'네가 원하는 게 어떤 거야, 그럼?'

'That white one / with the barred tail, / right in the
'저 하얀 놈이야 꼬리에 줄무늬가 있고,

middle of the flock.'
무리 가운데 있는.'

157

'Oh, / very well. Kill it / and take it with you.'
'아,   좋아.'   그걸 잡아서 가져가도록 해.'

Well, / I did what she said, / Mr. Holmes, / and I carried
음,   저는 누나 말대로 했습니다,   홈즈 씨,   그리고 거위를 갖고

the bird / all the way to Kilburn. I told my pal what I had
킬번으로 갔지요.   친구에게 제가 한 일을 말했죠,

done, / for he was a man / that it was easy to tell a thing
그 친구에겐   그런 일을 말하는 게 편했으니까요.

like that to. He laughed until he choked, / and we got a
그는 숨이 막힐 듯이 웃어댔고,   우리는 칼로

knife / and opened the goose. My heart turned to water, /
거위 배를 갈랐습니다.   저는 심장이 멎는 듯 했어요,

for there was no sign of the stone, / and I knew that some
왜냐하면 보석이 흔적도 없었거든요,

terrible mistake had occurred. I left the bird, / rushed
그래서 끔찍한 실수를 저질렀다는 걸 알았죠.   저는 거위를 놓고,

back to my sister's, / and hurried into the back yard.
누나 집으로 달려가서,   급히 뒷마당으로 향했습니다.

There was not a bird to be seen / there.
거위가 한 마리도 보이지 않았습니다   그곳에는.

Key Expression ?

조동사 would
다양한 의미로 사용되는 조동사 would의 대표적인 용법을 알아봅시다.

▶ will의 과거형 : 과거 짐작(~였을 것이다), 주어의 의지(~하려 했다)
▶ 불규칙한 과거 습관 : '~하곤 했다'
▶ 과거의 고집이나 의지 : 주로 not과 결합하여 '끝내 ~하지 않으려 했다'
▶ 정중한 부탁 : 의문문 'Would you ~?'의 형태로 '~해 주시겠어요?'

ex) Not one word would he tell me as to where they had gone.
그것들이 어디로 갔는지에 대해 그는 한 마디도 하지 않으려 했습니다.
If Horner were in danger it would be another thing.
만약 호너가 위험하다면 문제는 달랐겠지.

---

brand 낙인을 찍다

'Where are they all, / Maggie?' / I cried.
거위는 모두 어디 있어, 매기 누나?' 제가 소리쳤죠.

'Gone to the dealer's, / Jem.'
상인에게 갔지, 젬.'

'Which dealer's?'
어느 상인?'

'Breckinridge, / of Covent Garden.'
브렉킨리지야, 코벤트 가든에 있는.'

'But was there another / with a barred tail?' / I asked, /
그런데 또 있었어 꼬리에 줄무늬가 있는 놈이?' 제가 물었죠,

'the same as the one I chose?'
내가 고른 것과 똑같이 생긴 것 말이야?'

'Yes, Jem; / there were two barred-tailed ones, / and I
그래, 젬; 꼬리에 줄무늬가 있는 놈이 두 마리였는데,

could never tell them apart.'
나도 구별하기 힘들어.'

Well, then, / of course / I saw it all, / and I ran off
'그제서야, 물론 저는 모든 것을 알았고, 달려갔습니다

/ as hard as my feet would carry me / to this man
온 힘을 다해서 브레킨리지라는 남자에게;

Breckinridge; / but he had sold the lot / at once, / and
하지만 그는 그걸 팔아버렸고 즉시,

not one word would he tell me / as to where they had
한 마디도 하지 않으려 했습니다 어디에 팔았는지에 대해.

gone. You heard him yourselves / to-night. Well, / he has
당신도 들었겠지요 오늘 밤. 음

always answered me like that. My sister thinks / that I
그는 항상 그렇게 대답했습니다. 누나는 생각해요

am going mad. Sometimes / I think that I am myself.
제가 미쳤다고. 가끔 저도 그런 생각이 들어요.

And now / — and now / I am myself a branded thief, /
그리고 지금 — 지금 저는 도둑이라는 낙인이 찍히고 말았습니다,

without ever having touched the wealth / for which I sold
부를 만져보지도 못한 채 제 인격을 팔아서 산.

my character. God help me! God help me!"
오 하나님! 하나님 도와주세요!"

He burst into convulsive sobbing, / with his face buried
그는 발작적으로 흐느끼기 시작했다,   두 손에 얼굴을 묻은 채.

in his hands.

There was a long silence, / broken only by his heavy
긴 침묵이 흘렸고,   들리는 것은 그의 거친 숨소리와

breathing / and by the measured tapping of Sherlock
홈즈가 손가락으로 탁탁 두드리는 소리 뿐이었다

Holmes' finger-tips / upon the edge of the table. Then /
탁자 가장자리를.   그러다가

my friend rose / and threw open the door.
내 친구가 일어서서   문을 활짝 열었다.

"Get out!" / said he.
"나가게!"   그가 말했다.

"What, sir! Oh, Heaven bless you!"
"뭐라고요!   오, 감사합니다!"

"No more words. Get out!"
"더 이상 아무 말 말고.   나가게!"

Key Expression

명령문, and ~ : ~해라, 그러면~할 것이다

명령문에 and 혹은 아로 시작하는 문장을 덧붙여 결과를 나타낼 수 있습니다.
이때 명령문 부분은 if 조건문으로 바꾸어 쓸 수 있습니다.

▶ 명령문, and ~ : ~해라, 그러면 ~할 것이다.
  = If you ~, you will ~.
▶ 명령문, or ~ : ~해라, 그렇지 않으면 ~할 것이다.
  = If you don't ~, you will ~.

ex) Send him to jail now, and you make him a jail-bird for life.
  (=If you send him to jail now, you will make him a jail-bird for life.)
  지금 그를 감옥에 보내 보게, 그러면 그를 평생 감옥에 들락거리는 사람으로 만
  드는 게 되지.

---

convulsive 발작적인, 경련성인 | clatter 털커덕 소리를 내다 | crisp 바스락거리는 | rattle 덜컹거리다 | footfall
발소리 | after all 어쨌든 | retain (관계를) 보유하다 | deficiencies 부족 | commute 감형하다 | jail-bird
감옥을 제집 드나들 듯 하는 사람 | whimsical 기발한

And no more words were needed. There was a rush, /
그리고 더 이상 말은 필요 없었다.　　　　　　　급하게 달아나

a clatter upon the stairs, / the bang of a door, / and the
우당탕 계단을 내려가는 소리와,　　　문이 쾅 닫히고,

crisp rattle of running footfalls / from the street.
빠르게 뛰어가는 소리만 들릴 뿐이었다　　　거리에서.

"After all, / Watson," / said Holmes, / reaching up his
　"어쨌든,　　　왓슨,"　　홈즈가 말했다,　　파이프를 향해 손을 뻗으며,

hand for his clay pipe, / "I am not retained / by the
　　　　　　　　　　　　"난 관계를 맺은 것도 아니니까

police / to supply their deficiencies. If Horner were in
경찰에게　그들이 부족한 걸 채워 넣으라고.　　만약 호너가 위험하다면

danger / it would be another thing; / but this fellow will
문제는 달랐겠지;　　　　　하지만 이 자가 그에게 불리한

not appear against him, / and the case must collapse. I
증언을 하러 나타나진 않을 테고,　　그러면 사건은 틀림없이 기각될 테니까.

suppose / that I am commuting a felony, / but it is just
어쩌면　　내가 죄인을 풀어주고 말았을 수도 있지만,　　그게 어쩌면

possible / that I am saving a soul. This fellow will not
한 영혼을 구한 것일 수도 있지.　　이 자는 다시 죄를 짓지 않을 걸세;

go wrong again; / he is too terribly frightened. Send
무척 겁을 먹었으니.　　　　　지금 그를

him to jail now, / and you make him a jail-bird / for life.
감옥에 보내 보게,　　그러면 그를 감옥에 들락거리게 만드는 것이지　평생 동안.

Besides, / it is the season of forgiveness. Chance has put
게다가,　　지금은 용서의 계절이 아닌가.　　　　우연히 만났고

in our way / a most singular and whimsical problem, /
아주 이상하고 별난 사건을,

and its solution is its own reward. If you will have the
해결했으니 그것으로 보상이 되었네.

goodness to touch the bell, / Doctor, / we will begin
자네가 친절하게 초인종을 눌러 준다면,　　의사 양반,

another investigation, / in which, / also a bird will be the
우리는 또 다른 조사를 시작하겠지,　　그 일에서도,　　새가 주요한 특징이 될 테고 말이야."

chief feature."

mini test 6

A. 다음 문장을 해석해 보세요.

(1) Well, / the temptation of sudden wealth / so easily acquired / was too much for you, / as it has been for better men / before you.
→

(2) Suddenly / an idea came into my head / which showed me / how I could beat the best detective that ever lived.
→

(3) I am myself a branded thief, / without ever having touched the wealth / for which I sold my character.
→

(4) Chance has put in our way / a most singular and whimsical problem, / and its solution is its own reward.
→

B. 다음 주어진 문장이 되도록 빈칸에 써 넣으세요.

(1) 네놈이나 네놈 거위 얘긴 더 이상 못 참겠어.

→

(2) 당신이 방금 전에 저 상인에게 한 <u>질문을 우연히 듣고 말았어요.</u>

	which

you put to the salesman just now.

(3) 당신이 바로 제가 찾아 헤맸던 그분이군요.

→

(4) 그곳에는 새가 한 마리도 보이지 않았습니다.

→

A. (1) 그래, 그렇게 손쉽게 얻을 수 있는 돈벼락의 유혹이 너무 컸겠지, 자네 이전에 더 부자인 사람들에게 도 그랬으니까. (2) 갑자기 아무리 유능한 탐정이라도 속일 수 있는 생각이 머릿속에 떠올랐다. (3) 저는 제 영혼을 팔아서 얻은 부를 만져보지도 못한 채 도둑이라는 낙인이 찍히고 말았다. (4) 우연히 아주 이상하고

C. 다음 주어진 문구가 알맞은 문장이 되도록 순서를 맞추어 보세요.

(1) 그게 네놈이랑 무슨 상관이 있지?
[it / to / What / you / with / do / have]
→

(2) 제가 도움을 드릴 분이 도대체 누구신지 말해주시오.
[is / have / it / of / that / I / who / assisting / the pleasure]
Pray tell me _____.

(3) 정말로 약해 빠진 친구로군!
[a / is / What / it / shrimp]
_____, to be sure!

(4) 사건을 마무리 지으려면 그런 사소한 일도 확실히 해 두는 게 좋겠지.
[well / cleared / That / as / be / up / little / may]
_____ to make the
case complete.

D. 다음 단어에 대한 맞는 설명과 연결해 보세요.

(1) pester ▶ ◀ ① keep asking you to do something
(2) catastrophe ▶ ◀ ② honest or morally right
(3) scrupulous ▶ ◀ ③ push something quickly
(4) thrust ▶ ◀ ④ great suffering or damage

⟨The Five Orange Pips⟩

&

⟨The Adventure of the Blue Carbuncle⟩를

다시 읽어 보세요.

Episode 1

The Five Orange Pips

 1

When I glance over my notes and records of the Sherlock Holmes cases between the years '82 and '90, I am faced by so many which present strange and interesting features that it is no easy matter to know which to choose and which to leave. Some, however, have already gained publicity through the papers, and others have not offered a field for those peculiar qualities which my friend possessed in so high a degree, and which it is the object of these papers to illustrate. Some, too, have baffled his analytical skill, and would be, as narratives, beginnings without an ending, while others have been but partially cleared up, and have their explanations founded rather upon conjecture and surmise than on that absolute logical proof which was so dear to him. There is, however, one of these last which was so remarkable in its details and so startling in its results that I am tempted to give some account of it in spite of the fact that there are points in connection with it which never have been, and probably never will be, entirely cleared up.

The year '87 furnished us with a long series of cases of greater or less interest, of which I retain the records. Among my headings under this one twelve months I find an account of the adventure of the Paradol Chamber, of the Amateur Mendicant Society, who held a luxurious club in the lower vault of a furniture warehouse, of the facts connected with the loss of the British barque "Sophy Anderson", of the singular adventures of the Grice Patersons in the island of Uffa, and finally of the Camberwell poisoning case. In the latter, as may be remembered, Sherlock Holmes was able, by winding up the dead man's watch, to prove that it had been wound up two hours before, and that therefore the deceased had gone to bed within that time — a deduction which was of the greatest importance in clearing up the case. All these I may sketch out at some future date, but none of them present such singular features as the strange train of circumstances which I have now taken up my pen to describe.

It was in the latter days of September, and the equinoctial gales had set in with exceptional violence. All day the wind had screamed and the rain had beaten against the windows, so that even here in the heart of great, hand-made London we were forced to raise our minds for the instant from the routine of life and to recognise the presence of those great elemental forces which shriek at mankind through the bars of his civilisation, like untamed beasts in a cage. As evening drew in, the storm grew higher and louder, and the wind cried and sobbed like a child in the chimney. Sherlock Holmes sat moodily at one side of the fireplace cross-indexing his records of crime, while I at the other was deep in one of Clark Russell's fine sea-stories until the howl of the gale from without seemed to blend with the text, and the splash of the rain to lengthen out into the long swash of the sea waves. My wife was on a visit to her mother's, and for a few days I was a dweller once more in my old quarters at Baker Street.

"Why," said I, glancing up at my companion, "that was surely the bell. Who could come to-night? Some friend of yours, perhaps?"

"Except yourself I have none," he answered.

"I do not encourage visitors."

"A client, then?"

"If so, it is a serious case. Nothing less would bring a man out on such a day and at such an hour. But I take it that it is more likely to be some crony of the landlady's."

Sherlock Holmes was wrong in his conjecture, however, for there came a step in the passage and a tapping at the door. He stretched out his long arm to turn the lamp away from himself and towards the vacant chair upon which a newcomer must sit.

"Come in!" said he.

The man who entered was young, some two-and-twenty at the outside, well-groomed and trimly clad, with something of refinement and delicacy in his bearing. The streaming umbrella which he held in his hand, and his long shining waterproof told of the fierce weather through which he had come. He looked about him anxiously in the glare of the lamp, and I could see that his face was pale and his eyes heavy, like those of a man who is weighed down with some great anxiety.

"I owe you an apology," he said, raising his golden pince-nez to his eyes.

"I trust that I am not intruding. I fear that I have brought some traces of the storm and rain into your snug chamber."

"Give me your coat and umbrella," said Holmes.

"They may rest here on the hook and will be dry presently. You have come up from the south-west, I see."

"Yes, from Horsham."

"That clay and chalk mixture which I see upon your toe caps is quite distinctive."

"I have come for advice."

"That is easily got."

"And help."

"That is not always so easy."

"I have heard of you, Mr. Holmes. I heard from Major Prendergast how you saved him in the Tankerville Club scandal."

"Ah, of course. He was wrongfully accused of cheating at cards."

"He said that you could solve anything."

"He said too much."

"That you are never beaten."

"I have been beaten four times — three times by men, and once by a woman."

"But what is that compared with the number of your successes?"

"It is true that I have been generally successful."

"Then you may be so with me."

"I beg that you will draw your chair up to the fire and favour me with some details as to your case."

"It is no ordinary one."

"None of those which come to me are. I am the last court of appeal."

"And yet I question, sir, whether, in all your experience, you have ever listened to a more mysterious and inexplicable chain of events than those which have happened in my own family."

"You fill me with interest," said Holmes.

"Pray give us the essential facts from the commencement, and I can afterwards question you as to those details which seem to me to be most important."

The young man pulled his chair up and pushed his wet feet out towards the blaze.

"My name," said he, "is John Openshaw, but my own affairs have, as far as I can understand, little to do with this awful business. It is a hereditary matter; so in order to give you an idea of the facts, I must go back to the commencement of the affair.

You must know that my grandfather had two sons — my uncle Elias and my father Joseph. My father had a small factory at Coventry, which he enlarged at the time of the invention of bicycling. He was a patentee of the Openshaw unbreakable tire, and his business met with such success that he was able to sell it and to retire upon a handsome competence.

My uncle Elias emigrated to America when he was a young man and became a planter in Florida, where he was reported to have done very well. At the time of the war he fought in Jackson's army, and afterwards under Hood, where he rose to be a colonel. When Lee laid down his arms my uncle returned to his plantation, where he remained for three or four years. About 1869 or 1870 he came back to Europe and took a small estate in Sussex, near Horsham. He had made a very considerable fortune in the States, and his reason for leaving them was his aversion to the negroes, and his dislike of the Republican policy in extending the franchise to them.

He was a singular man, fierce and quick-tempered, very foul-mouthed when he was angry, and of a most retiring disposition. During all the years that he lived at Horsham, I doubt if ever he set foot in the town.

He had a garden and two or three fields round his house, and there he would take his exercise, though very often for weeks on end he would never leave his room. He drank a great deal of brandy and smoked very heavily, but he would see no society and did not want any friends, not even his own brother.

He didn't mind me; in fact, he took a fancy to me, for at the time when he saw me first I was a youngster of twelve or so. This would be in the year 1878, after he had been eight or nine years in England. He begged my father to let me live with him and he was very kind to me in his way. When he was sober he used to be fond of playing backgammon and draughts with me, and he would make me his representative both with the servants and with the tradespeople, so that by the time that I was sixteen I was quite master of the house.

I kept all the keys and could go where I liked and do what I liked, so long as I did not disturb him in his privacy. There was one singular exception, however, for he had a single room, a lumber-room up among the attics, which was invariably locked, and which he would never permit either me or anyone else to enter. With a boy's curiosity I have peeped through the keyhole, but I was never able to see more than such a collection of old trunks and bundles as would be expected in such a room.

One day — it was in March, 1883 — a letter with a foreign stamp lay upon the table in front of the colonel's plate. It was not a common thing for him to receive letters, for his bills were all paid in ready money, and he had no friends of any sort. 'From India!' said he as he took it up, 'Pondicherry postmark! What can this be?' Opening it hurriedly, out there jumped five little dried orange pips, which pattered down upon his plate. I began to laugh at this, but the laugh was struck from my lips at the sight of his face. His lip had fallen, his eyes were protruding, his skin the colour of putty, and he glared at the envelope which he still held in his trembling hand, 'K. K. K.!' he shrieked, and then, 'My God, my God, my sins have overtaken me!'

'What is it, uncle?' I cried.

'Death,' said he, and rising from the table he retired to his room, leaving me palpitating with horror. I took up the envelope and saw scrawled in red ink upon the inner flap, just above the gum, the letter K three times repeated. There was nothing else save the five dried pips. What could be the reason of his overpowering terror? I left the breakfast-table, and as I ascended the stair I met him coming down with an old rusty key, which must have belonged to the attic, in one hand, and a small brass box, like a cashbox, in the other.

'They may do what they like, but I'll checkmate them still,' said he with an oath.

'Tell Mary that I shall want a fire in my room to-day, and send down to Fordham, the Horsham lawyer.'

I did as he ordered, and when the lawyer arrived I was asked to step up to the room. The fire was burning brightly, and in the grate there was a mass of black, fluffy ashes, as of burned paper, while the brass box stood open and empty beside it. As I glanced at the box I noticed, with a start, that upon the lid was printed the treble K which I had read in the morning upon the envelope.

'I wish you, John,' said my uncle, 'to witness my will. I leave my estate, with all its advantages and all its disadvantages, to my brother, your father, whence it will, no doubt, descend to you. If you can enjoy it in peace, well and good! If you find you cannot, take my advice, my boy, and leave it to your deadliest enemy. I am sorry to give you such a two-edged thing, but I can't say what turn things are going to take. Kindly sign the paper where Mr. Fordham shows you.'

I signed the paper as directed, and the lawyer took it away with him. The singular incident made, as you may think, the deepest impression upon me, and I pondered over it and turned it every way in my mind without being able to make anything of it. Yet I could not shake off the vague feeling of dread which it left behind, though the sensation grew less keen as the weeks passed and nothing happened to disturb the usual routine of our lives. I could see a change in my uncle, however. He drank more than ever, and he was less inclined for any sort of society. Most of his time he would spend in his room, with the door locked upon the inside, but sometimes he would emerge in a sort of drunken frenzy and would burst out of the house and tear about the garden with a revolver in his hand, screaming out that he was afraid of no man, and that he was not to be cooped up, like a sheep in a pen, by man or devil. When these hot fits were over, however, he would rush tumultuously in at the door and lock and bar it behind him, like a man who can brazen it out no longer against the terror which lies at the roots of his soul. At such times I have seen his face, even on a cold day, glisten with moisture, as though it were new raised from a basin. Well, to come to an end of the matter, Mr. Holmes, and not to abuse your patience, there came a night when he made one of those drunken sallies from which he never came back. We found him, when we went to search for him, face downward in a little green-scummed pool, which lay at the foot of the garden. There was no sign of any violence, and the water was but two feet deep, so that the jury, having regard to his known eccentricity, brought in a verdict of 'suicide.' But I, who knew how he winced from the very thought of death, had much ado to persuade myself that he had gone out of his way to meet it. The matter passed, however, and my father entered into possession of the estate, and of some £14,000, which lay to his credit at the bank."

 2

"One moment," Holmes interposed, "your statement is, I foresee, one of the most remarkable to which I have ever listened. Let me have the date of the reception by your uncle of the letter, and the date of his supposed suicide."

"The letter arrived on March 10, 1883. His death was seven weeks later, upon the night of May 2nd."

"Thank you. Pray proceed."

"When my father took over the Horsham property, he, at my request, made a careful examination of the attic, which had been always locked up. We found the brass box there, although its contents had been destroyed. On the inside of the cover was a paper label, with the initials of K. K. K. repeated upon it, and 'Letters, memoranda, receipts, and a register' written beneath.

These, we presume, indicated the nature of the papers which had been destroyed by Colonel Openshaw. For the rest, there was nothing of much importance in the attic save a great many scattered papers and note-books bearing upon my uncle's life in America. Some of them were of the war time and showed that he had done his duty well and had borne the repute of a brave soldier. Others were of a date during the reconstruction of the Southern states, and were mostly concerned with politics, for he had evidently taken a strong part in opposing the carpet-bag politicians who had been sent down from the North.

Well, it was the beginning of '84 when my father came to live at Horsham, and all went as well as possible with us until the January of '85. On the fourth day after the new year I heard my father give a sharp cry of surprise as we sat together at the breakfast-table. There he was, sitting with a newly opened envelope in one hand and five dried orange pips in the outstretched palm of the other one. He had always laughed at what he called my cock-and-bull story about the colonel, but he looked very scared and puzzled now that the same thing had come upon himself.

'Why, what on earth does this mean, John?' he stammered.

My heart had turned to lead.

'It is K. K. K.,' said I.

He looked inside the envelope.

'So it is,' he cried.

'Here are the very letters. But what is this written above them?'

'Put the papers on the sundial,' I read, peeping over his shoulder.

'What papers? What sundial?' he asked.

'The sundial in the garden. There is no other,' said I; 'but the papers must be those that are destroyed.'

'Pooh!' said he, gripping hard at his courage.

'We are in a civilised land here, and we can't have tomfoolery of this kind. Where does the thing come from?'

'From Dundee,' I answered, glancing at the postmark.

'Some preposterous practical joke,' said he.

'What have I to do with sundials and papers? I shall take no notice of such nonsense.'

'I should certainly speak to the police,' I said.

'And be laughed at for my pains. Nothing of the sort.'

'Then let me do so?'

'No, I forbid you. I won't have a fuss made about such nonsense.'

It was in vain to argue with him, for he was a very obstinate man. I went about, however, with a heart which was full of forebodings. On the third day after the coming of the letter my father went from home to visit an old friend of his, Major Freebody, who is in command of one of the forts upon Portsdown Hill. I was glad that he should go, for it seemed to me that he was farther from danger when he was away from home. In that, however, I was in error. Upon the second day of his absence I received a telegram from the major, imploring me to come at once.

My father had fallen over one of the deep chalk-pits which abound in the neighbourhood, and was lying senseless, with a shattered skull. I hurried to him, but he passed away without having ever recovered his consciousness. He had, as it appears, been returning from Fareham in the twilight, and as the country was unknown to him, and the chalk-pit unfenced, the jury had no hesitation in bringing in a verdict of 'death from accidental causes.' Carefully as I examined every fact connected with his death, I was unable to find anything which could suggest the idea of murder. There were no signs of violence, no footmarks, no robbery, no record of strangers having been seen upon the roads. And yet I need not tell you that my mind was far from at ease, and that I was well-nigh certain that some foul plot had been woven round him.

In this sinister way I came into my inheritance. You will ask me why I did not dispose of it? I answer, because I was well convinced that our troubles were in some way dependent upon an incident in my uncle's life, and that the danger would be as pressing in one house as in another.

It was in January, '85, that my poor father met his end, and two years and eight months have elapsed since then. During that time I have lived happily at Horsham, and I had begun to hope that this curse had passed away from the family, and that it had ended with the last generation. I had begun to take comfort too soon, however; yesterday morning the blow fell in the very shape in which it had come upon my father."

The young man took from his waistcoat a crumpled envelope, and turning to the table he shook out upon it five little dried orange pips. "This is the envelope," he continued.

"The postmark is London — eastern division. Within are the very words which were upon my father's last message: 'K. K. K.'; and then 'Put the papers on the sundial.'"

"What have you done?" asked Holmes.

"Nothing."

"Nothing?"

"To tell the truth" — he sank his face into his thin, white hands — "I have felt helpless. I have felt like one of those poor rabbits when the snake is writhing towards it. I seem to be in the grasp of some resistless, inexorable evil, which no foresight and no precautions can guard against."

"Tut! Tut!" cried Sherlock Holmes.

"You must act, man, or you are lost. Nothing but energy can save you. This is no time for despair."

"I have seen the police."

"Ah!"

"But they listened to my story with a smile. I am convinced that the inspector has formed the opinion that the letters are all practical jokes, and that the deaths of my relations were really accidents, as the jury stated, and were not to be connected with the warnings."

Holmes shook his clenched hands in the air.

"Incredible imbecility!" he cried.

"They have, however, allowed me a policeman, who may remain in the house with me."

"Has he come with you to-night?"

"No. His orders were to stay in the house."

Again Holmes raved in the air.

"Why did you come to me," he cried, "and, above all, why did you not come at once?"

"I did not know. It was only to-day that I spoke to Major Prendergast about my troubles and was advised by him to come to you."

"It is really two days since you had the letter. We should have acted before this. You have no further evidence, I suppose, than that which you have placed before us — no suggestive detail which might help us?"

"There is one thing," said John Openshaw.

He rummaged in his coat pocket, and, drawing out a piece of discoloured, blue-tinted paper, he laid it out upon the table.

"I have some remembrance," said he, "that on the day when my uncle burned the papers I observed that the small, unburned margins which lay amid the ashes were of this particular colour. I found this single sheet upon the floor of his room, and I am inclined to think that it may be one of the papers which has, perhaps, fluttered out from among the others, and in that way has escaped destruction. Beyond the mention of pips, I do not see that it helps us much. I think myself that it is a page from some private diary. The writing is undoubtedly my uncle's."

Holmes moved the lamp, and we both bent over the sheet of paper, which showed by its ragged edge that it had indeed been torn from a book. It was headed, "March, 1869," and beneath were the following enigmatical notices:

4th. Hudson came. Same old platform.

7th. Set the pips on McCauley, Paramore, and John Swain, of St Augustine.

9th. McCauley cleared.

10th. John Swain cleared.

12th. Visited Paramore. All well.

"Thank you!" said Holmes, folding up the paper and returning it to our visitor.

"And now you must on no account lose another instant. We cannot spare time even to discuss what you have told me. You must get home instantly and act."

"What shall I do?"

"There is but one thing to do. It must be done at once. You must put this piece of paper which you have shown us into the brass box which you have described. You must also put in a note to say that all the other papers were burned by your uncle, and that this is the only one which remains. You must assert that in such words as will carry conviction with them. Having done this, you must at once put the box out upon the sundial, as directed. Do you understand?"

"Entirely."

"Do not think of revenge, or anything of the sort, at present. I think that we may gain that by means of the law; but we have our web to weave, while theirs is already woven. The first consideration is to remove the pressing danger which threatens you. The second is to clear up the mystery and to punish the guilty parties."

"I thank you," said the young man, rising and pulling on his overcoat.

"You have given me fresh life and hope. I shall certainly do as you advise."

"Do not lose an instant. And, above all, take care of yourself in the meanwhile, for I do not think that there can be a doubt that you are threatened by a very real and imminent danger. How do you go back?"

"By train from Waterloo."

"It is not yet nine. The streets will be crowded, so I trust that you may be in safety. And yet you cannot guard yourself too closely."

"I am armed."

"That is well. To-morrow I shall set to work upon your case."

"I shall see you at Horsham, then?"

"No, your secret lies in London. It is there that I shall seek it."

"Then I shall call upon you in a day, or in two days, with news as to the box and the papers. I shall take your advice in every particular."

He shook hands with us and took his leave. Outside the wind still screamed and the rain splashed and pattered against the windows. This strange, wild story seemed to have come to us from amid the mad elements — blown in upon us like a sheet of sea-weed in a gale — and now to have been reabsorbed by them once more.

Sherlock Holmes sat for some time in silence, with his head sunk forward and his eyes bent upon the red glow of the fire. Then he lit his pipe, and leaning back in his chair he watched the blue smoke-rings as they chased each other up to the ceiling.

"I think, Watson," he remarked at last, "that of all our cases we have had none more fantastic than this."

"Save, perhaps, the Sign of Four."

"Well, yes. Save, perhaps, that. And yet this John Openshaw seems to me to be walking amid even greater perils than did the Sholtos."

"But have you," I asked, "formed any definite conception as to what these perils are?"

"There can be no question as to their nature," he answered.

"Then what are they? Who is this K. K. K., and why does he pursue this unhappy family?"

Sherlock Holmes closed his eyes and placed his elbows upon the arms of his chair, with his finger-tips together.

"The ideal reasoner," he remarked, "would, when he had once been shown a single fact in all its bearings, deduce from it not only all the chain of events which led up to it but also all the results which would follow from it. As Cuvier could correctly describe a whole animal by the contemplation of a single bone, so the observer who has thoroughly understood one link in a series of incidents should be able to accurately state all the other ones, both before and after. We have not yet grasped the results which the reason alone can attain to. Problems may be solved in the study which have baffled all those who have sought a solution by the aid of their senses. To carry the art, however, to its highest pitch, it is necessary that the reasoner should be able to utilise all the facts which have come to his knowledge; and this in itself implies, as you will readily see, a possession of all knowledge, which, even in these days of free education and encyclopaedias, is a somewhat rare accomplishment. It is not so impossible, however, that a man should possess all knowledge which is likely to be useful to him in his work, and this I have endeavoured in my case to do. If I remember rightly, you on one occasion, in the early days of our friendship, defined my limits in a very precise fashion."

"Yes," I answered, laughing.

"It was a singular document. Philosophy, astronomy, and politics were marked at zero, I remember. Botany variable, geology profound as regards the mud-stains from any region within fifty miles of town, chemistry eccentric, anatomy unsystematic, sensational literature and crime records unique, violin-player, boxer, swordsman, lawyer, and self-poisoner by cocaine and tobacco. Those, I think, were the main points of my analysis."

Holmes grinned at the last item.

"Well," he said, "I say now, as I said then, that a man should keep his little brain-attic stocked with all the furniture that he is likely to use, and the rest he can put away in the lumber-room of his library, where he can get it if he wants it. Now, for such a case as the one which has been submitted to us to-night, we need certainly to muster all our resources. Kindly hand me down the letter K of the 'American Encyclopaedia' which stands upon the shelf beside you. Thank you. Now let us consider the situation and see what may be deduced from it. In the first place, we may start with a strong presumption that Colonel Openshaw had some very strong reason for leaving America. Men at his time of life do not change all their habits and exchange willingly the charming climate of Florida for the lonely life of an English provincial town. His extreme love of solitude in England suggests the idea that he was in fear of someone or something, so we may assume as a working hypothesis that it was fear of someone or something which drove him from America. As to what it was he feared, we can only deduce that by considering the formidable letters which were received by himself and his successors. Did you remark the postmarks of those letters?"

"The first was from Pondicherry, the second from Dundee, and the third from London."

"From East London. What do you deduce from that?"

"They are all seaports. That the writer was on board of a ship."

"Excellent. We have already a clue. There can be no doubt that the probability — the strong probability — is that the writer was on board of a ship. And now let us consider another point. In the case of Pondicherry, seven weeks elapsed between the threat and its fulfilment, in Dundee it was only some three or four days. Does that suggest anything?"

"A greater distance to travel."

"But the letter had also a greater distance to come."

"Then I do not see the point."

"There is at least a presumption that the vessel in which the man or men are is a sailing-ship. It looks as if they always send their singular warning or token before them when starting upon their mission. You see how quickly the deed followed the sign when it came from Dundee. If they had come from Pondicherry in a steamer they would have arrived almost as soon as their letter. But, as a matter of fact, seven weeks elapsed. I think that those seven weeks represented the difference between the mail-boat which brought the letter and the sailing vessel which brought the writer."

"It is possible."

"More than that. It is probable. And now you see the deadly urgency of this new case, and why I urged young Openshaw to caution. The blow has always fallen at the end of the time which it would take the senders to travel the distance. But this one comes from London, and therefore we cannot count upon delay."

"Good God!" I cried.

"What can it mean, this relentless persecution?"

"The papers which Openshaw carried are obviously of vital importance to the person or persons in the sailing-ship. I think that it is quite clear that there must be more than one of them. A single man could not have carried out two deaths in such a way as to deceive a coroner's jury. There must have been several in it, and they must have been men of resource and determination. Their papers they mean to have, be the holder of them who it may. In this way you see K. K. K. ceases to be the initials of an individual and becomes the badge of a society."

"But of what society?"

"Have you never —" said Sherlock Holmes, bending forward and sinking his voice — "have you never heard of the Ku Klux Klan?"

"I never have."

Holmes turned over the leaves of the book upon his knee.

"Here it is," said he presently:

"'Ku Klux Klan. A name derived from the fanciful resemblance to the sound produced by cocking a rifle. This terrible secret society was formed by some ex-Confederate soldiers in the Southern states after the Civil War, and it rapidly formed local branches in different parts of the country, notably in Tennessee, Louisiana, the Carolinas, Georgia, and Florida. Its power was used for political purposes, principally for the terrorising of the negro voters and the murdering and driving from the country of those who were opposed to its views. Its outrages were usually preceded by a warning sent to the marked man in some fantastic but generally recognised shape — a sprig of oak-leaves in some parts, melon seeds or orange pips in others. On receiving this the victim might either openly abjure his former ways, or might fly from the country. If he braved the matter out, death would unfailingly come upon him, and usually in some strange and unforeseen manner. So perfect was the organisation of the society, and so systematic its methods, that there is hardly a case upon record where any man succeeded in braving it with impunity, or in which any of its outrages were traced home to the perpetrators. For some years the organisation flourished in spite of the efforts of the United States government and of the better classes of the community in the South. Eventually, in the year 1869, the movement rather suddenly collapsed, although there have been sporadic outbreaks of the same sort since that date.'"

"You will observe," said Holmes, laying down the volume, "that the sudden breaking up of the society was coincident with the disappearance of Openshaw from America with their papers. It may well have been cause and effect. It is no wonder that he and his family have some of the more implacable spirits upon their track. You can understand that this register and diary may implicate some of the first men in the South, and that there may be many who will not sleep easy at night until it is recovered."

"Then the page we have seen —"

"Is such as we might expect. It ran, if I remember right, 'sent the pips to A, B, and C' — that is, sent the society's warning to them. Then there are successive entries that A and B cleared, or left the country, and finally that C was visited, with, I fear, a sinister result for C. Well, I think, Doctor, that we may let some light into this dark place, and I believe that the only chance young Openshaw has in the meantime is to do what I have told him. There is nothing more to be said or to be done to-night, so hand me over my violin and let us try to forget for half an hour the miserable weather and the still more miserable ways of our fellow-men."

 3

It had cleared in the morning, and the sun was shining with a subdued brightness through the dim veil which hangs over the great city. Sherlock Holmes was already at breakfast when I came down.

"You will excuse me for not waiting for you," said he; "I have, I foresee, a very busy day before me in looking into this case of young Openshaw's."

"What steps will you take?" I asked.

"It will very much depend upon the results of my first inquiries. I may have to go down to Horsham, after all."

"You will not go there first?"

"No, I shall commence with the City. Just ring the bell and the maid will bring up your coffee."

As I waited, I lifted the unopened newspaper from the table and glanced my eye over it. It rested upon a heading which sent a chill to my heart.

"Holmes," I cried, "you are too late."

"Ah!" said he, laying down his cup, "I feared as much. How was it done?"

He spoke calmly, but I could see that he was deeply moved.

"My eye caught the name of Openshaw, and the heading 'Tragedy Near Waterloo Bridge.' Here is the account:

Between nine and ten last night Police-Constable Cook, of the H Division, on duty near Waterloo Bridge, heard a cry for help and a splash in the water. The night, however, was extremely dark and stormy, so that, in spite of the help of several passers-by, it was quite impossible to effect a rescue. The alarm, however, was given, and, by the aid of the water-police, the body was eventually recovered. It proved to be that of a young gentleman whose name, as it appears from an envelope which was found in his pocket, was John Openshaw, and whose residence is near Horsham. It is conjectured that he may have been hurrying down to catch the last train from Waterloo Station, and that in his haste and the extreme darkness he missed his path and walked over the edge of one of the small landing-places for river steamboats. The body exhibited no traces of violence, and there can be no doubt that the deceased had been the victim of an unfortunate accident, which should have the effect of calling the attention of the authorities to the condition of the riverside landing-stages."

We sat in silence for some minutes, Holmes more depressed and shaken than I had ever seen him.

"That hurts my pride, Watson," he said at last.

"It is a petty feeling, no doubt, but it hurts my pride. It becomes a personal matter with me now, and, if God sends me health, I shall set my hand upon this gang. That he should come to me for help, and that I should send him away to his death — !"

He sprang from his chair and paced about the room in uncontrollable agitation, with a flush upon his sallow cheeks and a nervous clasping and unclasping of his long thin hands.

"They must be cunning devils," he exclaimed at last.

"How could they have decoyed him down there? The Embankment is not on the direct line to the station. The bridge, no doubt, was too crowded, even on such a night, for their purpose. Well, Watson, we shall see who will win in the long run. I am going out now!"

"To the police?"

"No; I shall be my own police. When I have spun the web they may take the flies, but not before."

All day I was engaged in my professional work, and it was late in the evening before I returned to Baker Street. Sherlock Holmes had not come back yet. It was nearly ten o'clock before he entered, looking pale and worn. He walked up to the sideboard, and tearing a piece from the loaf he devoured it voraciously, washing it down with a long draught of water.

"You are hungry," I remarked.

"Starving. It had escaped my memory. I have had nothing since breakfast."

"Nothing?"

"Not a bite. I had no time to think of it."

"And how have you succeeded?"

"Well."

"You have a clue?"

"I have them in the hollow of my hand. Young Openshaw shall not long remain unavenged. Why, Watson, let us put their own devilish trade-mark upon them. It is well thought of!"

"What do you mean?"

He took an orange from the cupboard, and tearing it to pieces he squeezed out the pips upon the table. Of these he took five and thrust them into an envelope. On the inside of the flap he wrote "S. H. for J. O." Then he sealed it and addressed it to "Captain James Calhoun, Barque Lone Star, Savannah, Georgia."

"That will await him when he enters port," said he, chuckling. "It may give him a sleepless night. He will find it as sure a precursor of his fate as Openshaw did before him."

"And who is this Captain Calhoun?"

"The leader of the gang. I shall have the others, but he first."

"How did you trace it, then?"

He took a large sheet of paper from his pocket, all covered with dates and names.

"I have spent the whole day," said he, "over Lloyd's registers and files of the old papers, following the future career of every vessel which touched at Pondicherry in January and February in '83. There were thirty-six ships of fair tonnage which were reported there during those months. Of these, one, the Lone Star, instantly attracted my attention, since, although it was reported as having cleared from London, the name is that which is given to one of the states of the Union."

"Texas, I think."

"I was not and am not sure which; but I knew that the ship must have an American origin."

"What then?"

"I searched the Dundee records, and when I found that the barque Lone Star was there in January, '85, my suspicion became a certainty. I then inquired as to the vessels which lay at present in the port of London."

"Yes?"

"The Lone Star had arrived here last week. I went down to the Albert Dock and found that she had been taken down the river by the early tide this morning, homeward bound to Savannah. I wired to Gravesend and learned that she had passed some time ago, and as the wind is easterly I have no doubt that she is now past the

Goodwins and not very far from the Isle of Wight."

"What will you do, then?"

"Oh, I have my hand upon him. He and the two mates, are as I learn, the only native-born Americans in the ship. The others are Finns and Germans. I know, also, that they were all three away from the ship last night. I had it from the stevedore who has been loading their cargo. By the time that their sailing-ship reaches Savannah the mail-boat will have carried this letter, and the cable will have informed the police of Savannah that these three gentlemen are badly wanted here upon a charge of murder."

There is ever a flaw, however, in the best laid of human plans, and the murderers of John Openshaw were never to receive the orange pips which would show them that another, as cunning and as resolute as themselves, was upon their track. Very long and very severe were the equinoctial gales that year. We waited long for news of the Lone Star of Savannah, but none ever reached us. We did at last hear that somewhere far out in the Atlantic a shattered stern-post of a boat was seen swinging in the trough of a wave, with the letters "L. S." carved upon it, and that is all which we shall ever know of the fate of the Lone Star.

The Adventure
of the Blue Carbuncle

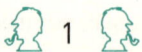 1

I had called upon my friend Sherlock Holmes upon the second morning after Christmas, with the intention of wishing him the compliments of the season. He was lounging upon the sofa in a purple dressing-gown, a pipe-rack within his reach upon the right, and a pile of crumpled morning papers, evidently newly studied, near at hand. Beside the couch was a wooden chair, and on the angle of the back hung a very seedy and disreputable hard-felt hat, much the worse for wear, and cracked in several places. A lens and a forceps lying upon the seat of the chair suggested that the hat had been suspended in this manner for the purpose of examination.

"You are engaged," said I; "perhaps I interrupt you."

"Not at all. I am glad to have a friend with whom I can discuss my results. The matter is a perfectly trivial one" — he jerked his thumb in the direction of the old hat — "but there are points in connection with it which are not entirely devoid of interest and even of instruction."

I seated myself in his armchair and warmed my hands before his crackling fire, for a sharp frost had set in, and the windows were thick with the ice crystals.

"I suppose," I remarked, "that, homely as it looks, this thing has some deadly story linked on to it — that it is the clue which will guide you in the solution of some mystery and the punishment of some crime."

"No, no. No crime," said Sherlock Holmes, laughing.

"Only one of those whimsical little incidents which will happen when you have four million human beings all jostling each other within the space of a few square miles. Amid the action and reaction of so dense a swarm of humanity, every possible combination of events may be expected to take place, and many a little problem will be presented which may be striking and bizarre without being criminal. We have already had experience of such."

"So much so," I remarked, "that of the last six cases which I have added to my notes, three have been entirely free of any legal crime."

"Precisely. You allude to my attempt to recover the Irene Adler papers, to the singular case of Miss Mary Sutherland, and to the adventure of the man with the twisted lip. Well, I have no doubt that this small matter will fall into the same innocent category. You know Peterson, the commissionaire?"

"Yes."

"It is to him that this trophy belongs."

"It is his hat."

"No, no, he found it. Its owner is unknown. I beg that you will look upon it not as a battered billycock but as an intellectual problem. And, first, as to how it came here. It arrived upon Christmas morning, in company with a good fat goose, which is, I have no doubt, roasting at this moment in front of Peterson's fire. The facts are these: about four o'clock on Christmas morning, Peterson, who, as you know, is a very honest fellow, was returning from some small jollification and was making his way homeward down Tottenham Court Road. In front of him he saw, in the gaslight, a tallish man, walking with a slight stagger, and carrying a white goose slung over his shoulder. As he reached the corner of Goodge Street, a row broke out between this stranger and a little knot of roughs. One of the latter knocked off the man's hat, on which he raised his stick to defend himself and, swinging it over his head, smashed the shop window behind him. Peterson had rushed forward to protect the stranger from his assailants; but the man, shocked at having broken the window, and seeing an official-looking person in uniform rushing towards him, dropped his goose, took to his heels, and vanished amid the labyrinth of small streets which lie at the back of Tottenham Court Road. The roughs had also fled at the appearance of Peterson, so that he was left in possession of the field of battle, and also of the spoils of victory in the shape of this battered hat and a most unimpeachable Christmas goose."

"Which surely he restored to their owner?"

"My dear fellow, there lies the problem. It is true that 'For Mrs. Henry Baker' was printed upon a small card which was tied to the bird's left leg, and it is also true that the initials 'H. B.' are legible upon the lining of this hat, but as there are some thousands of Bakers, and some hundreds of Henry Bakers in this city of ours, it is not easy to restore lost property to any one of them."

"What, then, did Peterson do?"

"He brought round both hat and goose to me on Christmas morning, knowing that even the smallest problems are of interest to me. The goose we retained until this morning, when there were signs that, in spite of the slight frost, it would be well that it should be eaten without unnecessary delay. Its finder has carried it off, therefore, to fulfil the ultimate destiny of a goose, while I continue to retain the hat of the unknown gentleman who lost his Christmas dinner."

"Did he not advertise?"

"No."

"Then, what clue could you have as to his identity?"

"Only as much as we can deduce."

"From his hat?"

"Precisely."

"But you are joking. What can you gather from this old battered felt?"

"Here is my lens. You know my methods. What can you gather yourself as to the individuality of the man who has worn this article?"

I took the tattered object in my hands and turned it over rather ruefully. It was a very ordinary black hat of the usual round shape, hard and much the worse for wear. The lining had been of red silk, but was a good deal discoloured. There was no maker's name; but, as Holmes had remarked, the initials "H. B." were scrawled upon one side. It was pierced in the brim for a hat-securer, but the elastic was missing. For the rest, it was cracked, exceedingly dusty, and spotted in several places, although there seemed to have been some attempt to hide the discoloured patches by smearing them with ink. "I can see nothing," said I, handing it back to my friend.

"On the contrary, Watson, you can see everything. You fail, however, to reason from what you see. You are too timid in drawing your inferences."

"Then, pray tell me what it is that you can infer from this hat?" He picked it up and gazed at it in the peculiar introspective fashion which was characteristic of him.

"It is perhaps less suggestive than it might have been," he remarked, "and yet there are a few inferences which are very distinct, and a few others which represent at least a strong balance of probability. That the man was highly intellectual is of course obvious upon the face of it, and also that he was fairly well-to-do within the last three years, although he has now fallen upon evil days. He had foresight, but has less now than formerly, pointing to a moral retrogression, which, when taken with the decline of his fortunes, seems to indicate some evil influence, probably drink, at work upon him. This may account also for the obvious fact that his wife has ceased to love him."

"My dear Holmes!"

"He has, however, retained some degree of self-respect," he continued, disregarding my remonstrance.

"He is a man who leads a sedentary life, goes out little, is out of training entirely, is middle-aged, has grizzled hair which he has had cut within the last few days, and which he anoints with lime-cream. These are the more patent facts which are to be deduced from his hat. Also, by the way, that it is extremely improbable that he has gas laid on in his house."

"You are certainly joking, Holmes."

"Not in the least. Is it possible that even now, when I give you these results, you are unable to see how they are attained?"

"I have no doubt that I am very stupid, but I must confess that I am unable to follow you. For example, how did you deduce that this man was intellectual?"

For answer Holmes clapped the hat upon his head. It came right over the forehead and settled upon the bridge of his nose.

"It is a question of cubic capacity," said he; "a man with so large a brain must have something in it."

"The decline of his fortunes, then?"

"This hat is three years old. These flat brims curled at the edge came in then. It is a hat of the very best quality. Look at the band of ribbed silk and the excellent lining. If this man could afford to buy so expensive a hat three years ago, and has had no hat since, then he has assuredly gone down in the world."

"Well, that is clear enough, certainly. But how about the foresight and the moral retrogression?"

Sherlock Holmes laughed.

"Here is the foresight," said he putting his finger upon the little disc and loop of the hat-securer.

"They are never sold upon hats. If this man ordered one, it is a sign of a certain amount of foresight, since he went out of his way to take this precaution against the wind. But since we see that he has broken the elastic and has not troubled to replace it, it is obvious that he has less foresight now than formerly, which is a distinct proof of a weakening nature. On the other hand, he has endeavoured to conceal some of these stains upon the felt by daubing them with ink, which is a sign that he has not entirely lost his self-respect."

"Your reasoning is certainly plausible."

"The further points, that he is middle-aged, that his hair is grizzled, that it has been recently cut, and that he uses lime-cream, are all to be gathered from a close examination of the lower part of the lining. The lens discloses a large number of hair-ends, clean cut by the scissors of the barber. They all appear to be adhesive, and there is a distinct odour of lime-cream. This dust, you will observe, is not the gritty, grey dust of the street but the fluffy brown dust of the house, showing that it has been hung up indoors most of the time, while the marks of moisture upon the inside are proof positive that the wearer perspired very freely, and could therefore, hardly be in the best of training."

"But his wife — you said that she had ceased to love him."

"This hat has not been brushed for weeks. When I see you, my dear Watson, with a week's accumulation of dust upon your hat, and when your wife allows you to go out in such a state, I shall fear that you also have been unfortunate enough to lose your wife's affection."

"But he might be a bachelor."

"Nay, he was bringing home the goose as a peace-offering to his wife. Remember the card upon the bird's leg."

"You have an answer to everything. But how on earth do you deduce that the gas is not laid on in his house?"

"One tallow stain, or even two, might come by chance; but when I see no less than five, I think that there can be little doubt that the individual must be brought into frequent contact with burning tallow — walks upstairs at night probably with his hat in one hand and a guttering candle in the other. Anyhow, he never got tallow-stains from a gas-jet. Are you satisfied?"

"Well, it is very ingenious," said I, laughing; "but since, as you said just now, there has been no crime committed, and no harm done save the loss of a goose, all this seems to be rather a waste of energy."

Sherlock Holmes had opened his mouth to reply, when the door flew open, and Peterson, the commissionaire, rushed into the apartment with flushed cheeks and the face of a man who is dazed with astonishment.

"The goose, Mr. Holmes! The goose, sir!" he gasped.

"Eh? What of it, then? Has it returned to life and flapped off through the kitchen window?"

Holmes twisted himself round upon the sofa to get a fairer view of the man's excited face.

"See here, sir! See what my wife found in its crop!"

He held out his hand and displayed upon the centre of the palm a brilliantly scintillating blue stone, rather smaller than a bean in size, but of such purity and radiance that it twinkled like an electric point in the dark hollow of his hand.

Sherlock Holmes sat up with a whistle.

"By Jove, Peterson!" said he, "this is treasure trove indeed. I suppose you know what you have got?"

"A diamond, sir? A precious stone. It cuts into glass as though it were putty."

"It's more than a precious stone. It is the precious stone."

"Not the Countess of Morcar's blue carbuncle!" I ejaculated.

"Precisely so. I ought to know its size and shape, seeing that I have read the advertisement about it in The Times every day lately. It is absolutely unique, and its value can only be conjectured, but the reward offered of £1000 is certainly not within a twentieth part of the market price."

"A thousand pounds! Great Lord of mercy!"

The commissionaire plumped down into a chair and stared from one to the other of us.

"That is the reward, and I have reason to know that there are sentimental considerations in the background which would induce the Countess to part with half her fortune if she could but recover the gem."

"It was lost, if I remember aright, at the Hotel Cosmopolitan," I remarked.

"Precisely so, on December 22nd, just five days ago. John Horner, a plumber, was accused of having abstracted it from the lady's jewel-case. The evidence against him was so strong that the case has been referred to the Assizes. I have some account of the matter here, I believe."

He rummaged amid his newspapers, glancing over the dates, until at last he smoothed one out, doubled it over, and read the following paragraph:

"Hotel Cosmopolitan Jewel Robbery. John Horner, 26, plumber, was brought up upon the charge of having upon the 22nd inst., abstracted from the jewel-case of the Countess of Morcar the valuable gem known as the blue carbuncle. James Ryder, upper-attendant at the hotel, gave his evidence to the effect that he had shown Horner up to the dressing-room of the Countess of Morcar upon the day of the robbery in order that he might solder the second bar of the grate, which was loose. He had remained with Horner some little time, but had finally been called away. On returning, he found that Horner had disappeared, that the bureau had been forced open, and that the small morocco casket in which, as it afterwards transpired, the Countess was accustomed to keep her jewel, was lying empty upon the dressing-table. Ryder instantly gave the alarm, and Horner was arrested the same evening; but the stone could not be found either upon his person or in his rooms. Catherine Cusack, maid to the Countess, deposed to having heard Ryder's cry of dismay on discovering the robbery, and to having rushed into the room, where she found matters as described by the last witness. Inspector Bradstreet, B division, gave evidence as to the arrest of Horner, who struggled frantically, and protested his innocence in the strongest terms. Evidence of a previous conviction for robbery having been given against the prisoner, the magistrate refused to deal summarily with the offence, but referred it to the Assizes. Horner, who had shown signs of intense emotion during the proceedings, fainted away at the conclusion and was carried out of court."

"Hum! So much for the police-court," said Holmes thoughtfully, tossing aside the paper.

"The question for us now to solve is the sequence of events leading from a rifled jewel-case at one end to the crop of a goose in Tottenham Court Road at the other. You see, Watson, our little deductions have suddenly assumed a much more important and less innocent aspect. Here is the stone; the stone came from the goose, and the goose came from Mr. Henry Baker, the gentleman with the bad hat and all the other characteristics with which I have bored you. So now we must set ourselves very seriously to finding this gentleman and ascertaining what part he has played in this little mystery. To do this, we must try the simplest means first, and these lie undoubtedly in an advertisement in all the evening papers. If this fail, I shall have recourse to other methods."

"What will you say?"

"Give me a pencil and that slip of paper. Now, then: 'Found at the corner of Goodge Street, a goose and a black felt hat. Mr. Henry Baker can have the same by applying at 6.30 this evening at 221b, Baker Street.' That is clear and concise."

"Very. But will he see it?"

"Well, he is sure to keep an eye on the papers, since, to a poor man, the loss was a heavy one. He was clearly so scared by his mischance in breaking the window and by the approach of Peterson that he thought of nothing but flight, but since then he must have bitterly regretted the impulse which caused him to drop his bird. Then, again, the introduction of his name will cause him to see it, for everyone who knows him will direct his attention to it. Here you are, Peterson, run down to the advertising agency and have this put in the evening papers."

"In which, sir?"

"Oh, in the Globe, Star, Pall Mall, St. James's, Evening News, Standard, Echo, and any others that occur to you."

"Very well, sir. And this stone?"

"Ah, yes, I shall keep the stone. Thank you. And, I say, Peterson, just buy a goose on your way back and leave it here with me, for we must have one to give to this gentleman in place of the one which your family is now devouring."

When the commissionaire had gone, Holmes took up the stone and held it against the light.

"It's a bonny thing," said he.

"Just see how it glints and sparkles. Of course it is a nucleus and focus of crime. Every good stone is. They are the devil's pet baits. In the larger and older jewels every facet may stand for a bloody deed. This stone is not yet twenty years old. It was found in the banks of the Amoy River in southern China and is remarkable in having every characteristic of the carbuncle, save that it is blue in shade instead of ruby red. In spite of its youth, it has already a sinister history. There have been two murders, a vitriol-throwing, a suicide, and several robberies brought about for the sake of this forty-grain weight of crystallised charcoal. Who would think that so pretty a toy would be a purveyor to the gallows and the prison? I'll lock it up in my strong box now and drop a line to the Countess to say that we have it."

"Do you think that this man Horner is innocent?"

"I cannot tell."

"Well, then, do you imagine that this other one, Henry Baker, had anything to do with the matter?"

"It is, I think, much more likely that Henry Baker is an absolutely innocent man, who had no idea that the bird which he was carrying was of considerably more value than if it were made of solid gold. That, however, I shall determine by a very simple test if we have an answer to our advertisement."

"And can you do nothing until then?"

"Nothing."

"In that case I shall continue my professional round. But I shall come back in the evening at the hour you have mentioned, for I should like to see the solution of so tangled a business."

"Very glad to see you. I dine at seven. There is a woodcock, I believe. By the way, in view of recent occurrences, perhaps I ought to ask Mrs. Hudson to examine its crop."

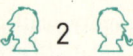

I had been delayed at a case, and it was a little after half-past six when I found myself in Baker Street once more. As I approached the house I saw a tall man in a Scotch bonnet with a coat which was buttoned up to his chin waiting outside in the bright semicircle which was thrown from the fanlight. Just as I arrived the door was opened, and we were shown up together to Holmes' room.

"Mr. Henry Baker, I believe," said he, rising from his armchair and greeting his visitor with the easy air of geniality which he could so readily assume.

"Pray take this chair by the fire, Mr. Baker. It is a cold night, and I observe that your circulation is more adapted for summer than for winter. Ah, Watson, you have just come at the right time. Is that your hat, Mr. Baker?"

"Yes, sir, that is undoubtedly my hat."

He was a large man with rounded shoulders, a massive head, and a broad, intelligent face, sloping down to a pointed beard of grizzled brown. A touch of red in nose and cheeks, with a slight tremor of his extended hand, recalled Holmes' surmise as to his habits. His rusty black frock-coat was buttoned right up in front, with the collar turned up, and his lank wrists protruded from his sleeves without a sign of cuff or shirt. He spoke in a slow staccato fashion, choosing his words with care, and gave the impression generally of a man of learning and letters who had had ill-usage at the hands of fortune.

"We have retained these things for some days," said Holmes, "because we expected to see an advertisement from you giving your address. I am at a loss to know now why you did not advertise."

Our visitor gave a rather shamefaced laugh.

"Shillings have not been so plentiful with me as they once were," he remarked.

"I had no doubt that the gang of roughs who assaulted me had carried off both my hat and the bird. I did not care to spend more money in a hopeless attempt at recovering them."

"Very naturally. By the way, about the bird, we were compelled to eat it."

"To eat it!"

Our visitor half rose from his chair in his excitement.

"Yes, it would have been of no use to anyone had we not done so. But I presume that this other goose upon the sideboard, which is about the same weight and perfectly fresh, will answer your purpose equally well?"

"Oh, certainly, certainly," answered Mr. Baker with a sigh of relief.

"Of course, we still have the feathers, legs, crop, and so on of your own bird, so if you wish — "

The man burst into a hearty laugh.

"They might be useful to me as relics of my adventure," said he, "but beyond that I can hardly see what use the disjecta membra of my late acquaintance are going to be to me. No, sir, I think that, with your permission, I will confine my attentions to the excellent bird which I perceive upon the sideboard."

Sherlock Holmes glanced sharply across at me with a slight shrug of his shoulders.

"There is your hat, then, and there your bird," said he.

"By the way, would it bore you to tell me where you got the other one from? I am somewhat of a fowl fancier, and I have seldom seen a better grown goose."

"Certainly, sir," said Baker, who had risen and tucked his newly gained property under his arm.

"There are a few of us who frequent the Alpha Inn, near the Museum — we are to be found in the Museum itself during the day, you understand. This year our good host, Windigate by name, instituted a goose club, by which, on consideration of some few pence every week, we were each to receive a bird at Christmas. My pence were duly paid, and the rest is familiar to you. I am much indebted to you, sir, for a Scotch bonnet is fitted neither to my years nor my gravity."

With a comical pomposity of manner he bowed solemnly to both of us and strode off upon his way.

"So much for Mr. Henry Baker," said Holmes when he had closed the door behind him.

"It is quite certain that he knows nothing whatever about the matter. Are you hungry, Watson?"

"Not particularly."

"Then I suggest that we turn our dinner into a supper and follow up this clue while it is still hot."

"By all means."

It was a bitter night, so we drew on our ulsters and wrapped cravats about our throats. Outside, the stars were shining coldly in a cloudless sky, and the breath of the passers-by blew out into smoke like so many pistol shots. Our footfalls rang out crisply and loudly as we swung through the doctors' quarter, Wimpole Street, Harley Street, and so through Wigmore Street into Oxford Street. In a quarter of an hour we were in Bloomsbury at the Alpha Inn, which is a small public-house at the corner of one of the streets which runs down into Holborn. Holmes pushed open the door of the private bar and ordered two glasses of beer from the ruddy-faced, white-aproned landlord.

"Your beer should be excellent if it is as good as your geese," said he.

"My geese!"

The man seemed surprised.

"Yes. I was speaking only half an hour ago to Mr. Henry Baker, who was a member of your goose club."

"Ah! Yes, I see. But you see, sir, them's not our geese."

"Indeed! Whose, then?"

"Well, I got the two dozen from a salesman in Covent Garden."

"Indeed? I know some of them. Which was it?"

"Breckinridge is his name."

"Ah! I don't know him. Well, here's your good health landlord, and prosperity to your house. Good-night."

"Now for Mr. Breckinridge," he continued, buttoning up his coat as we came out into the frosty air.

"Remember, Watson that though we have so homely a thing as a goose at one end of this chain, we have at the other a man who will certainly get seven years' penal servitude unless we can establish his innocence. It is possible that our inquiry may but confirm his guilt; but, in any case, we have a line of investigation which has been missed by the police, and which a singular chance has placed in our hands. Let us follow it out to the bitter end. Faces to the south, then, and quick march!"

We passed across Holborn, down Endell Street, and so through a zigzag of slums to Covent Garden Market. One of the largest stalls bore the name of Breckinridge upon it, and the proprietor a horsey-looking man, with a sharp face and trim side-whiskers was helping a boy to put up the shutters.

"Good-evening. It's a cold night," said Holmes.

The salesman nodded and shot a questioning glance at my companion.

"Sold out of geese, I see," continued Holmes, pointing at the bare slabs of marble.

"Let you have five hundred to-morrow morning."

"That's no good."

"Well, there are some on the stall with the gas-flare."

"Ah, but I was recommended to you."

"Who by?"

"The landlord of the Alpha."

"Oh, yes; I sent him a couple of dozen."

"Fine birds they were, too. Now where did you get them from?"

To my surprise the question provoked a burst of anger from the salesman.

"Now, then, mister," said he, with his head cocked and his arms akimbo, "what are you driving at? Let's have it straight, now."

"It is straight enough. I should like to know who sold you the geese which you supplied to the Alpha."

"Well then, I shan't tell you. So now!"

"Oh, it is a matter of no importance; but I don't know why you should be so warm over such a trifle."

"Warm! You'd be as warm, maybe, if you were as pestered as I am. When I pay good money for a good article there should be an end of the business; but it's 'Where are the geese?' and 'Who did you sell the geese to?' and 'What will you take for the geese?' One would think they were the only geese in the world, to hear the fuss that is made over them."

"Well, I have no connection with any other people who have been making inquiries," said Holmes carelessly.

"If you won't tell us the bet is off, that is all. But I'm always ready to back my opinion on a matter of fowls, and I have a fiver on it that the bird I ate is country bred."

"Well, then, you've lost your fiver, for it's town bred," snapped the salesman.

"It's nothing of the kind."

"I say it is."

"I don't believe it."

"D'you think you know more about fowls than I, who have handled them ever since I was a nipper? I tell you, all those birds that went to the Alpha were town bred."

"You'll never persuade me to believe that."

"Will you bet, then?"

"It's merely taking your money, for I know that I am right. But I'll have a sovereign on with you, just to teach you not to be obstinate."

The salesman chuckled grimly.

"Bring me the books, Bill," said he.

The small boy brought round a small thin volume and a great greasy-backed one, laying them out together beneath the hanging lamp.

"Now then, Mr. Cocksure," said the salesman, "I thought that I was out of geese, but before I finish you'll find that there is still one left in my shop. You see this little book?"

"Well?"

"That's the list of the folk from whom I buy. D'you see? Well, then, here on this page are the country folk, and the numbers after their names are where their accounts are in the big ledger. Now, then!

You see this other page in red ink? Well, that is a list of my town suppliers. Now, look at that third name. Just read it out to me."

"Mrs. Oakshott, 117, Brixton Road — 249," read Holmes.

"Quite so. Now turn that up in the ledger."

Holmes turned to the page indicated.

"Here you are, 'Mrs. Oakshott, 117, Brixton Road, egg and poultry supplier.' "

"Now, then, what's the last entry?"

"'December 22nd. Twenty-four geese at 7s. 6d.' /"

"Quite so. There you are. And underneath?"

"'Sold to Mr. Windigate of the Alpha, at 12s.' "

"What have you to say now?"

Sherlock Holmes looked deeply chagrined. He drew a sovereign from his pocket and threw it down upon the slab, turning away with the air of a man whose disgust is too deep for words. A few yards off he stopped under a lamp-post and laughed in the hearty, noiseless fashion which was peculiar to him.

"When you see a man with whiskers of that cut and the 'Pink 'un' protruding out of his pocket, you can always draw him by a bet," said he.

"I daresay that if I had put £100 down in front of him, that man would not have given me such complete information as was drawn from him by the idea that he was doing me on a wager. Well, Watson, we are, I fancy, nearing the end of our quest, and the only point which remains to be determined is whether we should go on to this Mrs. Oakshott to-night, or whether we should reserve it for to-morrow. It is clear from what that surly fellow said that there are others besides ourselves who are anxious about the matter, and I should — "

3

His remarks were suddenly cut short by a loud hubbub which broke out from the stall which we had just left. Turning round we saw a little rat-faced fellow standing in the centre of the circle of yellow light which was thrown by the swinging lamp, while Breckinridge, the salesman, framed in the door of his stall, was shaking his fists fiercely at the cringing figure.

"I've had enough of you and your geese," he shouted.

"I wish you were all at the devil together. If you come pestering me any more with your silly talk I'll set the dog at you. You bring Mrs. Oakshott here and I'll answer her, but what have you to do with it? Did I buy the geese off you?"

"No; but one of them was mine all the same," whined the little man.

"Well, then, ask Mrs. Oakshott for it."

"She told me to ask you."

"Well, you can ask the King of Proosia, for all I care. I've had enough of it. Get out of this!"

He rushed fiercely forward, and the inquirer flitted away into the darkness.

"Ha! This may save us a visit to Brixton Road," whispered Holmes. "Come with me, and we will see what is to be made of this fellow." Striding through the scattered knots of people who lounged round the flaring stalls, my companion speedily overtook the little man and touched him upon the shoulder. He sprang round, and I could see in the gas-light that every vestige of colour had been driven from his face.

"Who are you, then? What do you want?" he asked in a quavering voice.

"You will excuse me," said Holmes blandly, "but I could not help overhearing the questions which you put to the salesman just now. I think that I could be of assistance to you."

"You? Who are you? How could you know anything of the matter?"

"My name is Sherlock Holmes. It is my business to know what other people don't know."

"But you can know nothing of this?"

"Excuse me, I know everything of it. You are endeavouring to trace some geese which were sold by Mrs. Oakshott, of Brixton Road, to a salesman named Breckinridge, by him in turn to Mr. Windigate, of the Alpha, and by him to his club, of which Mr. Henry Baker is a member."

"Oh, sir, you are the very man whom I have longed to meet," cried the little fellow with outstretched hands and quivering fingers.

"I can hardly explain to you how interested I am in this matter." Sherlock Holmes hailed a four-wheeler which was passing.

"In that case we had better discuss it in a cosy room rather than in this wind-swept market-place," said he.

"But pray tell me, before we go farther, who it is that I have the pleasure of assisting."

The man hesitated for an instant.

"My name is John Robinson," he answered with a sidelong glance.

"No, no; the real name," said Holmes sweetly.

"It is always awkward doing business with an alias."

A flush sprang to the white cheeks of the stranger.

"Well then," said he, "my real name is James Ryder."

"Precisely so. Head attendant at the Hotel Cosmopolitan. Pray step into the cab, and I shall soon be able to tell you everything which you would wish to know."

The little man stood glancing from one to the other of us with half-frightened, half-hopeful eyes, as one who is not sure whether he is on the verge of a windfall or of a catastrophe. Then he stepped into the cab, and in half an hour we were back in the sitting-room at Baker Street. Nothing had been said during our drive, but the high, thin breathing of our new companion, and the claspings and unclaspings of his hands, spoke of the nervous tension within him.

"Here we are!" said Holmes cheerily as we filed into the room.

"The fire looks very seasonable in this weather. You look cold, Mr. Ryder. Pray take the basket-chair. I will just put on my slippers before we settle this little matter of yours. Now, then! You want to know what became of those geese?"

"Yes, sir."

"Or rather, I fancy, of that goose. It was one bird, I imagine in which you were interested — white, with a black bar across the tail."

Ryder quivered with emotion.

"Oh, sir," he cried, "can you tell me where it went to?"

"It came here."

"Here?"

"Yes, and a most remarkable bird it proved. I don't wonder that you should take an interest in it. It laid an egg after it was dead — the bonniest, brightest little blue egg that ever was seen. I have it here in my museum."

Our visitor staggered to his feet and clutched the mantelpiece with his right hand. Holmes unlocked his strong-box and held up the blue carbuncle, which shone out like a star, with a cold, brilliant, many-pointed radiance. Ryder stood glaring with a drawn face, uncertain whether to claim or to disown it.

"The game's up, Ryder," said Holmes quietly.

"Hold up, man, or you'll be into the fire! Give him an arm back into his chair, Watson. He's not got blood enough to go in for felony with impunity. Give him a dash of brandy. So! Now he looks a little more human. What a shrimp it is, to be sure!"

For a moment he had staggered and nearly fallen, but the brandy brought a tinge of colour into his cheeks, and he sat staring with frightened eyes at his accuser.

"I have almost every link in my hands, and all the proofs which I could possibly need, so there is little which you need tell me. Still, that little may as well be cleared up to make the case complete. You had heard, Ryder, of this blue stone of the Countess of Morcar's?"

"It was Catherine Cusack who told me of it," said he in a crackling voice.

"I see — her ladyship's waiting-maid. Well, the temptation of sudden wealth so easily acquired was too much for you, as it has been for better men before you; but you were not very scrupulous in the means you used. It seems to me, Ryder, that there is the making of a very pretty villain in you. You knew that this man Horner, the plumber, had been concerned in some such matter before, and that suspicion would rest the more readily upon him. What did you do, then? You made some small job in my lady's room — you and your confederate Cusack — and you managed that he should be the man sent for. Then, when he had left, you rifled the jewel-case, raised the alarm, and had this unfortunate man arrested. You then —"

Ryder threw himself down suddenly upon the rug and clutched at my companion's knees.

"For God's sake, have mercy!" he shrieked.

"Think of my father! Of my mother! It would break their hearts. I never went wrong before! I never will again. I swear it. I'll swear it on a Bible. Oh, don't bring it into court! For Christ's sake, don't!"

"Get back into your chair!" said Holmes sternly.

"It is very well to cringe and crawl now, but you thought little enough of this poor Horner in the dock for a crime of which he knew nothing."

"I will fly, Mr. Holmes. I will leave the country, sir. Then the charge against him will break down."

"Hum! We will talk about that. And now let us hear a true account of the next act. How came the stone into the goose, and how came the goose into the open market? Tell us the truth, for there lies your only hope of safety."

Ryder passed his tongue over his parched lips.

"I will tell you it just as it happened, sir," said he. "When Horner had been arrested, it seemed to me that it would be best for me to get away with the stone at once, for I did not know at what moment the police might not take it into their heads to search me and my room. There was no place about the hotel where it would be safe. I went out, as if on some commission, and I made for my sister's house. She had married a man named Oakshott, and lived in Brixton Road, where she fattened fowls for the market.

All the way there every man I met seemed to me to be a policeman or a detective; and, for all that it was a cold night, the sweat was pouring down my face before I came to the Brixton Road. My sister asked me what was the matter, and why I was so pale; but I told her that I had been upset by the jewel robbery at the hotel. Then I went into the back yard and smoked a pipe and wondered what it would be best to do.

I had a friend once called Maudsley, who went to the bad, and has just been serving his time in Pentonville. One day he had met me, and fell into talk about the ways of thieves, and how they could get rid of what they stole. I knew that he would be true to me, for I knew one or two things about him; so I made up my mind to go right on to Kilburn, where he lived, and take him into my confidence. He would show me how to turn the stone into money. But how to get to him in safety? I thought of the agonies I had gone through in coming from the hotel. I might at any moment be seized and searched, and there would be the stone in my waistcoat pocket. I was leaning against the wall at the time and looking at the geese which were waddling about round my feet, and suddenly an idea came into my head which showed me how I could beat the best detective that ever lived.

My sister had told me some weeks before that I might have the pick of her geese for a Christmas present, and I knew that she was always as good as her word. I would take my goose now, and in it I would carry my stone to Kilburn. There was a little shed in the yard, and behind this I drove one of the birds — a fine big one, white, with a barred tail. I caught it, and prying its bill open, I thrust the stone down its throat as far as my finger could reach. The bird gave a gulp, and I felt the stone pass along its gullet and down into its crop. But the creature flapped and struggled, and out came my sister to know what was the matter. As I turned to speak to her the brute broke loose and fluttered off among the others.

'Whatever were you doing with that bird, Jem?' says she.

'Well,' said I, 'you said you'd give me one for Christmas, and I was feeling which was the fattest.'

'Oh,' says she, 'we've set yours aside for you — Jem's bird, we call it. It's the big white one over yonder. There's twenty-six of them, which makes one for you, and one for us, and two dozen for the market.'

'Thank you, Maggie,' says I; 'but if it is all the same to you, I'd rather have that one I was handling just now.'

'The other is a good three pound heavier,' said she, 'and we fattened it expressly for you.'

'Never mind. I'll have the other, and I'll take it now,' said I.

'Oh, just as you like,' said she, a little huffed. 'Which is it you want, then?'

'That white one with the barred tail, right in the middle of the flock.'

'Oh, very well. Kill it and take it with you.'

Well, I did what she said, Mr. Holmes, and I carried the bird all the way to Kilburn. I told my pal what I had done, for he was a man that it was easy to tell a thing like that to. He laughed until he choked, and we got a knife and opened the goose. My heart turned to water, for there was no sign of the stone, and I knew that some terrible mistake had occurred. I left the bird, rushed back to my sister's, and hurried into the back yard. There was not a bird to be seen there.

'Where are they all, Maggie?' I cried.

'Gone to the dealer's, Jem.'

'Which dealer's?'

'Breckinridge, of Covent Garden.'

'But was there another with a barred tail?' I asked, 'the same as the one I chose?'

'Yes, Jem; there were two barred-tailed ones, and I could never tell them apart.'

Well, then, of course I saw it all, and I ran off as hard as my feet would carry me to this man Breckinridge; but he had sold the lot at once, and not one word would he tell me as to where they had gone. You heard him yourselves to-night. Well, he has always answered me like that. My sister thinks that I am going mad. Sometimes I think that I am myself. And now — and now I am myself a branded thief, without ever having touched the wealth for which I sold my character. God help me! God help me!"

He burst into convulsive sobbing, with his face buried in his hands.

There was a long silence, broken only by his heavy breathing and by the measured tapping of Sherlock Holmes' finger-tips upon the edge of the table. Then my friend rose and threw open the door.

"Get out!" said he.

"What, sir! Oh, Heaven bless you!"

"No more words. Get out!"

And no more words were needed. There was a rush, a clatter upon the stairs, the bang of a door, and the crisp rattle of running footfalls from the street.

"After all, Watson," said Holmes, reaching up his hand for his clay pipe, "I am not retained by the police to supply their deficiencies. If Horner were in danger it would be another thing; but this fellow will not appear against him, and the case must collapse. I suppose that I am commuting a felony, but it is just possible that I am saving a soul. This fellow will not go wrong again; he is too terribly frightened. Send him to jail now, and you make him a jail-bird for life. Besides, it is the season of forgiveness. Chance has put in our way a most singular and whimsical problem, and its solution is its own reward. If you will have the goodness to touch the bell, Doctor, we will begin another investigation, in which, also a bird will be the chief feature."